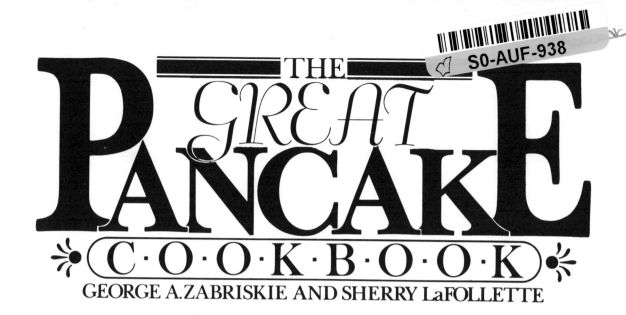

THE GREAT PANCAKE COOKBOOK

GEORGE A. ZABRISKIE AND SHERRY LaFOLLETTE

CONTEMPORARY
BOOKS, INC.
CHICAGO

Library of Congress Cataloging in Publication Data

Zabriskie, George A.
    The great pancake cookbook.

    Includes index.
    1. Pancakes, waffles, etc.   I. LaFollette, Sherry.
    II. Title.
TX770.Z32   1985   641.8   85-5712
ISBN 0-8092-5392-5

Published by Contemporary Books, Inc.
180 North Michigan Avenue, Chicago, Illinois 60601
Manufactured in the United States of America
Library of Congress Catalog Card Number: 85-5712
International Standard Book Number: 0-8092-5392-5

Published simultaneously in Canada by Beaverbooks, Ltd.
195 Allstate Parkway, Valleywood Business Park
Markham, Ontario L3R 4T8 Canada

CONTENTS

II. FROM GRIDDLE
    TO TABLE:

Using Add-Ins, Fillings,

INTRODUCTION

The American kitchen is returning to simple, down-home cooking. It is all part of the "back to basics" philosophy that is the trend of our times. Pancakes are the ultimate "back to basics" kind of food. Pancakes are simple and immediate. Whip up a batter. Drop some on a hot surface. Cook only a minute or two . . . then enjoy. That's all there is to it. Anyone can do it.

Hoe cakes were cooked by American pioneers on the flat blades of their hoes held over a fire. Even today there is something especially delicious about pancakes cooked out-of-doors over an open fire.

Indoors or out, pancakes are as American as apple pie. But unlike apple pie,

they are also English, French, Italian, Russian, Chinese, African, and practically every other nationality you care to mention. Pancakes are so basic—they are universal in both their heritage and their appeal.

Pancakes can be served with toppings, they can be used to enfold other foods, or other foods can be incorporated directly into the batter. With this versatility, pancakes can be served for breakfast, for lunch, as hors d'oeuvres, as a main course dish, or as a dessert.

Pancakes of one sort or another have been made in the kitchens of practically every culture in the world. Though they go by dozens of different names, they are all basically pancakes. The recipes in this book encompass traditional pancakes, our own variations of the traditional (with less fat and sodium, no added salt, and less sugar, or simpler preparation procedures), and some of our own invention. All provide delicious, nutritious food that is quick and easy to prepare—but that is just a bit out of the ordinary.

To fit our definition, a pancake must be made with a batter that is dropped on a hot flat surface: a griddle, soapstone, frying pan, or skillet. Further, the batter must contain a sizeable proportion of flour (egg batter foods like frittatas and omelettes are outside the scope of this book). However, anything that fits the above description is, in our opinion, a pancake. There are a few exceptions: the Chinese mandarin pancake, the Mexican tortilla, and the Indian chappati look like pancakes and are cooked like pancakes, but they are made from a dough—not a batter—that is patted, pressed, or rolled into very thin discs before being placed on the hot cooking surface. The original Americans, when they came over the ice from Asia, perhaps brought this unique kind of pancake with them. If so, then the pancake is very old, indeed—ten to fifteen thousand years old. Since they are in the same family, we have included recipes for making batter-based substitutes.

We have no way of knowing how our ancient ancestors prepared their pancakes—probably the batter was simply ground meal mixed with water, and was cooked on a hot surface of either stone or metal. However, by looking at recipes in nineteenth-century cookbooks, we do know how our more immediate ancestors prepared their pancakes—and also how far we have come in making the process simpler and more healthful.

The following recipe is from *The Official Handbook for the National Training School for Cookery*, published in London by Chapman and Hall in 1879.

LESSON NO. 4: PANCAKES

1. We take three ounces of flour and put it in a basin.

2. We add half a saltspoonful of salt, and mix it well into the flour.

3. We break two eggs into the flour and add a dessertspoonful of milk, and mix well together with a wooden spoon.

4. We stir in gradually half a pint of milk, making the mixture very smooth.

5. We put a frying pan on the fire, and put into it a piece of lard the size of a nut, and let it get quite hot, but it must not burn.

6. We then pour into the frying pan two large tablespoonsful of the batter, and let it run all over the pan.

7. When the pancake has become a light brown on one side, we should shake the pan and toss the pancake over, to brown the other side the same.

8. We should stand a plate on the hot plate, or in the front of the fire to heat.

9. When the pancake is fried, we turn it onto this heated plate.

10. We should squeeze about 15 drops of lemon juice, and sprinkle a teaspoonful of moist sugar over it.

11. We now roll up the pancake, and place it on the edge of the plate, so as to leave room for the remainder of the pancakes.

12. For serving we arrange the pancakes on a hot dish, placing one on top of the other.

Now it is finished.

After going through those dozen steps, *you* may be finished with pancakes forever. Take heart—here is a simple recipe from *Miss Corson's Practical American Cookery*, published by Dodd, Mead and Company in 1886.

Nearly all American breakfasts include some form of hot fried cakes with syrup or sugar.

ARMY SLAPJACKS

Dissolve two teaspoonsful of salt in a pint of cold water, mix the water smoothly with a tablespoonful of flour, and beat the mixture until it foams, then mix into it enough flour to make a rather thin batter. Fry the slapjacks in a hot frying pan, rubbed with a piece of raw fat salt pork or with a small piece of butter tied in a bit of clean cloth. If the frying pan is not smooth, the cakes will stick to it; therefore clean it by washing and wiping it thoroughly, and then rubbing it with dry salt.

That is all history. We don't prepare *our* batters this way and don't suggest that *you* do either.

ABOUT BATTERS

A properly made pancake very quickly turns a runny liquid into a solid food that is good to eat and good for you. To be good on both counts, pancakes must be light and easy to digest. Anyone who has experienced heavy pancakes knows they are usually quite thick and rubbery in texture. With enough butter and syrup, they may go down the gullet rather easily—but that's as far as they go. They sit there partially digested, reminding you of their presence for far too long a time. Heavy pancakes are that way because (a) the batter is old and all the leavening has gone out of it; (b) the batter is made so thick that it can't be cooked through before the outer surface begins to char; or (c) a combination of both of the above.

There are three basic ways to make light pancakes. You can make them very thin; you can add a leavening agent to the batter that will release carbon dioxide; or you can make a batter that con-

3

tains air. French crepes and Chinese mandarin pancakes are light because they are very thin. Most other pancakes are light because they are made with baking powder or baking soda plus an acid ingredient like buttermilk or sour cream, or are made with yeast. These various leavening ingredients cause carbon dioxide gas to be produced in the batter, lightening the cake and forming the bubbles that let you know when to turn the pancake over. Air in the batter will also produce a light pancake. Egg whites, beaten well and then folded into the batter, entrap air in their froth and make a very light pancake.

If you are a person who doesn't want to wait for the yeast to rise and you are on a very strict low-sodium and low-cholesterol diet (baking powders and sodas contain sodium, eggs contain cholesterol), we have discovered still another way to make light pancakes. Replace all liquids, eggs, and leavening with an equal amount of bottled carbonated water. Make sure that the bottle is freshly opened and therefore fully charged; also, check the label to be sure the bottled water contains no salt or other sodium compounds. You must use this batter right after it is mixed or the carbonation will escape.

The recipes that follow call for making a batter that is one of three different consistencies: *thin*—about the consistency of light cream; *normal*—about the consistency of heavy cream; or *thick*—about the consistency of melted ice cream.

ADDED INGREDIENTS

Preparing the batter is only the start of the pancake story. A large variety of ingredients can be added to the batter and cooked along with it. We call these *add-ins*. Pancakes can also be rolled or folded to enclose other ingredients, both sweet and savory. We call these *fillings*. Pancakes can be layered with still other kinds of ingredients; or syrups, spreads, and sauces can be applied to pancakes, both individually and stacked. The different ways that pancakes can be prepared is limited only by your creativity and your urge to experiment.

Experimenting is half the fun of any kind of cooking. Use your imagination: try preparing batters, add-ins, and fillings of your own invention. Pancakes do not require a high degree of expertise or precision in their preparation. Anyone who can beat up a batter and heat up a pan can serve up a platter of tasty, nutritious pancakes. And the more you put of your own ideas into the process, the more satisfied you will be with the result.

Before we began to write about food, we had the good fortune to live and work in many parts of this world. And as filmmakers, we were involved with a variety of peoples, cultures, and cuisines. From the start, we came to appreciate both the differences and the similarities in the way people prepare their food. In one form or another the pancake is almost universal. The simplest flour and water mix, and the most complex crepe, are only variations on the same theme; flat, round food that can be rolled, stacked, stuffed, and filled in an infinite variety of ways. In the stuffing and filling recipes we have drawn heavily on our travel experiences: Egyptian tabbouleh shows up as an added ingredient in a batter recipe—South American empanada fillings are wrapped in a pancake instead of a pastry shell—the flavors of a Black Forest torte manifest themselves layered in a stack of pancakes. When it comes to pancakes, the possibilities are endless.

THE PAN

Pancakes can be cooked on a hot rock, if it is flat enough. Since the beginning of cooking, probably more pancakes have been cooked this way than any other. Nineteenth-century cookbooks often cite a soapstone griddle as the preferred utensil for preparing pancakes, since it provides the two basic requirements for cooking perfect pancakes: uniform heat distribution and a nonstick surface. However, soapstone griddles are hard to come by in the twentieth century, so most of us have to get by with steel, iron,

or aluminum griddles or skillets. Generally, the heavier the pan, the more even the heat distribution will be. We use a well-seasoned old cast iron skillet. A seasoned surface is important, so that a minimum of oil or margarine will be required to keep the pancake from sticking to the pan during cooking. Pans with nonstick surfaces are very useful, but they are often made of relatively thin steel or aluminum and are not so good when it comes to even heat distribution. If you have an electric stove with a large element about the same size as the bottom of your pan, then there is no problem. Even if you do your cooking with gas there is a simple solution: During the cooking process, move the pan slowly in a circular motion over the flame to ensure even heating. Since pancakes have been popular camp-out food since the beginning, and since cast iron is heavy to carry and is likely to break if dropped on a hard place, most contemporary campers prefer lightweight, nonstick skillets. Just move the pan around over the flame and you can make perfect pancakes; or wait to cook them until the fire burns down to nice, even-heating coals.

A recent development in pancake cookery is the electric crepe maker. Initially, we thought of this device as simply a plug-in frying pan—just one more electrified utensil to clutter up the kitchen. A friend of ours, Eve Thomson—an ex-

5

tremely efficient real estate executive—was appalled that we would reject this state-of-the-art equipment in favor of a cast iron pan that you had to tilt and turn to make pancakes come out right. Rather than try to persuade us, Eve simply bought an electric crepe maker and gave it to us. We skeptics have been converted. The pan is a delight to use and makes thinner, lighter, more perfect crepes than we can turn out in our old fry pan.

The technique is a complete reversal of normal pancake cooking. Instead of putting the batter in the pan, you put the pan in the batter. The crepe maker consists of a heating element programmed to cycle on and off to keep the temperature just right for making crepes. The cooking surface at first glance appears to be the top of a conventional-looking crepe pan, with a gentle convex curve to it but with no handle. To produce crepes with this utensil you simply plug it in, wait for the light to come on, dip the cooking surface in the batter, remove it, turn it right side up for a few moments, then turn it upside down again and, with a slight nudge,

slip the cooked crepe onto a plate. The whole process takes about 30 seconds!

Any of our thin batter recipes will work well with the crepe maker by adding 2 tablespoons of melted butter or margarine to the batter and eliminating any vegetable oil in the recipe. Just follow the directions that come with the utensil and you should be able to produce extemely light, thin, tasty crepes from the start.

All the recipes in this book are designed to serve four persons; however, our recipe for four persons may satisfy only two or three hearty pancake eaters. Since these recipes can very easily be doubled, or tripled, or cut in half, we will leave the actual amount you make up to you.

Also, we do not give batter preparation times. However, none of the recipes for batters or doughs should take more than 5 minutes to prepare. Some fillings and toppings may take you a little longer, but pancake-making should be a quick and easy process. To that end, we have developed this book—full of uncomplicated recipes that we hope you will read, use, and enjoy.

I
BASIC PANCAKES

1
TIPS
AND
TECHNIQUES

Anyone who can boil water or fry an egg can prepare pancakes. People of all ages, with practically no kitchen equipment (and often no kitchen), have been doing it for centuries. Don't worry about not having the right pan, or the right food processor, or even the right ingredients. Pancakes are a very forgiving food. Almost any mix of good ingredients that can be poured onto a hot, greased surface will cook up into a surprisingly edible pancake. For obtaining the best results, however, we can offer a few tips based on our experience:

1. The cooking surface should be quite hot. A drop of water splattered on it should dance and hiss and disappear in a puff of steam.

2. The cooking surface should be a smooth, nonstick surface, either a prepared coating or greased (with margarine). If your pan has the former, use the plastic or wooden spatulas recommended by the manufacturer. Metal utensils will scratch and damage the prepared surface.

3. Because we employ some unusual ingredients in our batters, particularly the add-ins, give a quick stir to the batter before each batch is spooned into the pan. Add-in ingredients tend to settle out and can end up mostly in the last pancake—not a fair distribution since, in our experience, the chef usually consumes the last pancake.

4. Batters can be stored in your refrigerator in a tightly sealed jar. However, normal and thick batters tend to lose their lightness. The air or the carbon dioxide escapes and the pancakes become heavier and less desirable. Thin batters can be refrigerated successfully for a few days since they contain no leavening agents, but all of these batters are so simple, quick, and easy to make, it hardly seems worth the effort.

ABOUT FREEZING

Some people freeze pancakes, but again it is really easier to make them up fresh than to freeze and defrost them. However, a case can be made for freezing filled pancakes that are going to be reheated, anyway.

Prepare a double or triple batch and place in containers that can withstand the environments of both oven and freezer. If preparing for reheating in a conventional oven, disposable aluminum pans, ceramic pans, and even glass pans can be used. However, make sure ceramic and glass pans are marked both oven- and freezer-proof. Prepare these dishes exactly as you would if you were going to place them directly in the oven. Instead, cover them tightly with aluminum foil and, if they are warm or hot, let them cool to room temperature before placing them in the freezer.

To prepare for serving, place the foil-wrapped dish in a preheated 400°F. oven and cook for about 40 minutes, or until heated through. Since smaller containers may take less time, and larger ones more, lift off the foil and check the food after about 30 minutes. If the food appears to be heated through, leave the foil off and cook for another 5–10 minutes. If the food is not heated through, replace the foil and recheck at 10-minute intervals.

To reheat in the microwave, follow your manufacturer's instructions.

11

2
NORMAL BATTERS

Normal batter pancakes are the ones you will find most familiar—especially since prepared mixes are of this consistency. So first we'll explore how to make the best pancakes from prepared mixes—and then move on to a variety of pancakes made with different flours and combinations of flours. These pancakes are made with basic all-purpose flour, whole wheat flour, oats, cornmeal, rice, and bread crumbs—and with water, milk, yogurt, buttermilk, sour cream, and beer.

PREPARED MIXES

Although we haven't tried *all* the prepared pancake mixes currently available in the United States, we have tried those sold in the supermarkets in the New York City area.

By following the directions on the box, you can produce very satisfactory American-type breakfast pancakes. When buying prepared mixes, get those products that contain no preservatives or artificial coloring agents and as few sodium compounds (including salt) as possible. By law, the ingredients are listed on the box in order, with the largest quantity ingredient listed first and least quantity ingredient listed last. An acceptable product should have artificial ingredients and sodium compounds only at the very bottom of the list.

To improve any mix, try making pancakes with some of our add-in ingredients (see page 53) or with some of our toppings (see page 51). However, to have the most fun making pancakes, do it all yourself! Take our recipes, try them, experiment with them, change them. Use your imagination! That's the way to pancake pleasure.

BASIC GRIDDLE CAKES

Before the days of prepared mixes, this was the kind of pancake that was produced on commerical kitchen griddles in diners, restaurants, and hotel coffee shops all across America. It is still a good basic pancake—that you can improve with a variety of add-ins (see page 53) or toppings (see page 51).

1 cup all-purpose flour
1 teaspoon baking powder
1 tablespoon salad oil or melted
  shortening
1 egg
1 cup milk or water

1. Mix dry ingredients in a bowl.
2. Combine liquid ingredients together and beat well.

3. Combine the two mixtures together and blend briefly.

4. Pour about ¼ cup batter onto a lightly greased hot pan. Cook until many bubbles appear and top surface becomes set, about 1 minute. Turn over and cook the other side until pancake is done through the center, also about 1 minute.

Makes about 8 6-inch pancakes

13

BITS AND BREW CAKES

We said that we weren't going to have any yeast-rising recipes in this book. This recipe does use yeast as a leavening agent, but only in its reincarnation as beer. The brew not only lightens the cake but imparts its own distinctive flavor as well. These pancakes are not really made for breakfast or dessert, but with the added ingredients given below they go down very well as a hearty lunch. See page 53, Add-Ins, for other suggestions.

1 cup whole wheat flour
1¼ cups beer (add more as needed for
  normal batter consistency)
2 eggs, well beaten
⅓ cup coarsely grated cheddar cheese
½ cup diced ham
2 tablespoons Dijon mustard

1. Combine all ingredients in a bowl and mix well.

2. Pour about ¼ cup batter onto a lightly greased hot pan. When bubbles appear on the surface, turn pancakes over and cook on the other side, cooking a minute or more on each side.

Makes about 12 6-inch pancakes

CORN DOODLES

*I*n nineteenth-century America, a doodle was a trifle, something simple and small; so corn doodles were little, easy-to-make corn pancakes. With less liquid, they were often dropped into a kettle of hot fat, like doughnuts, but we prefer to prepare them as pancakes. They can be eaten out of hand just as they come off the fire, or served with a variety of toppings for breakfast or dessert (see page 51, Toppings).

½ cup cornmeal
½ cup whole wheat flour
2 tablespoons molasses
1 teaspoon baking powder
½ teaspoon allspice
1 egg
2 cups milk or water

1. Combine all ingredients in a bowl and mix well.

2. Drop about 2 tablespoons of batter onto a lightly greased hot pan. When bubbles form on top, turn over and cook the other side.

Makes about 12 3-inch doodles

14

PUMPKIN PANCAKES

*T*his is a versatile, all-American pancake. It can be served for breakfast topped with syrup, for lunch with sour cream, or for dessert with a rum and lemon sauce (see page 51), Toppings). You can also separate the egg, folding in the white at the last minute to produce small, fluffy pumpkin pancakes—an elegant variation.

1 cup canned pumpkin
¼ cup whole wheat or all-purpose
    flour
¾ cup milk or water
½ teaspoon cinnamon powder
¼ teaspoon ground cloves
2 tablespoons brown sugar
1 teaspoon baking powder
1 egg

1. Combine all ingredients in a bowl and mix well (you can use a blender).

2. Drop about ¼ cup of batter onto a lightly greased hot pan. When many bubbles appear, turn the pancake over and cook briefly on the other side.

Makes about 8 6-inch pancakes

INDIAN SLAPJACKS

Since native American Indians knew neither chickens or cows, these pancakes must have come along after the colonists settled in the New World. In any case, Indian slapjacks make a hearty, nourishing meal any time of the day. With some topping spooned on, they are even better (see page 51).

¾ cup cornmeal
1 cup hot milk
2 tablespoons maple syrup or molasses
2 eggs, beaten to a froth

1. Add the cornmeal slowly to the hot milk in a bowl. Stir continuously to avoid lumps. Once all the cornmeal is mixed in, stir vigorously and add the syrup.

2. In a separate bowl, beat the eggs to a froth and then combine with the cornmeal mixture. (Frothy eggs are necessary for light pancakes.)

3. Pour about ¼ cup of batter onto a lightly greased hot pan. After about a minute or so, turn and cook on the other side. The slapjacks should be cooked through the center.

Makes about 8 6-inch pancakes

15

HOT CEREAL CAKES

Come wintertime, and millions of Americans prepare hot cereals (such as oats) to get themselves going in the morning. These prepared cereals, usually containing no salts or preservatives, can be the basis for a whole spectrum of hearty pancakes, either made fresh or from leftovers. Because the cereals naturally produce more bulk than flour does, these pancakes are perfect for cooking with fruits, nuts, and other add-ins (see page 53).

2 cups hot cereal, prepared according
    to the directions on the box
2 eggs, well beaten
½ cup berries, diced fruit, nuts, or
    whatever pleases you (optional)

1. Combine prepared cereal and eggs in a bowl and mix well.

2. Add fruit or nuts if desired.

3. Pour about ¼ cup of batter onto a well-greased hot pan. Cook for about 2–3 minutes, until the edges of the pancakes are crispy. Turn and cook for a little less time on the other side.

Makes about 8 6-inch pancakes

OLD-FASHIONED FLAPJACKS

*T*his is the classic American breakfast pancake—big, but light, nutritious, and pleasing. It has a peculiar history. "Jack" is an eighteenth-century provincial English term for a half-cup liquid measure. A "flapjack" was a half cup of stewed fruits enclosed in a pastry flap and fried. In colonial America things were simplified—chopped fruit or berries were mixed into a batter and fried. Over time, the fruit often got left out and "flapjack" became just another name for pancake. These are good any way you fix them, but with fresh blueberries, or other fruit add-ins, they are exceptional (see page 53).

1 egg
1 cup milk
1 cup whole wheat flour or all-purpose flour
1 teaspoon baking powder
½ cup blueberries or other small or chopped fruit

1. Beat egg and milk together. Mix flour and baking powder together in a bowl.

2. Add liquid ingredients and fruit to the flour mixture and mix together quickly, only enough to make a pourable batter.

3. Pour about ¼ cup batter onto a lightly greased hot pan. Cook until many bubbles appear and top surface becomes set. Turn over and cook the other side until pancake is done through the center.

Makes about 8 6-inch pancakes

16

RICE PANCAKES

*T*his is an inventive and efficient way to utilize a little leftover rice. These crispy cakes can be served at breakfast with toppings (see page 51), or they can be used as you would use a potato pancake with an entrée.

1 cup boiled rice, freshly made or
  leftover
1 cup all-purpose flour
1 teaspoon baking powder
2 eggs, well beaten
1 scant cup of milk or water

1. Mix the dry ingredients together in a bowl. Add the eggs and milk and blend well.

2. Spoon about 2 tablespoons of the batter onto a well-greased hot pan. Cook until the edges of the rice cakes are crisp and brown. Turn over and cook about the same length of time on the other side.

Makes about 12 3-inch pancakes

SCANDINAVIAN SPINACH CAKES

*I*n the north country where the growing season is short and the tillable land in short supply, people tend to stretch their vegetables as much as possible. This use of chopped raw spinach makes an unusually wholesome and delicious luncheon pancake. You can also use it like a crepe to enfold other foods.

1 cup chopped fresh spinach
¾ cup whole wheat flour
½ teaspoon baking powder
½ cup yogurt
½ cup water
1 egg

1. Combine all ingredients in a bowl and mix well.

2. Drop about ¼ cup batter onto a lightly greased hot pan. When bubbles appear, turn the pancake over and cook on the other side, cooking about a minute on each side.

Makes about 8 6-inch pancakes

17

SOUR CREAM CAKES

*T*his is one of our favorite pancakes. Crispy around the edges and creamy in the middle, they offer a unique variety of tastes and textures. We especially like them served as a light lunch with Lebanese tabbouleh added to the batter (see page 53, Add-Ins).

½ cup whole wheat or all-purpose
 flour
½ cup bread crumbs
½ teaspoon baking powder
1 tablespoon vegetable oil
1 egg
⅓ cup sour cream
¾ cup water
1 cup tabbouleh (optional)

1. Combine dry ingredients in a bowl and mix well.

2. Combine oil, egg, sour cream, and water and beat well, then add to the dry ingredients and mix well. Add tabbouleh, if desired.

3. Spoon about 2 tablespoons of the batter onto a well-greased hot pan. When the edges of the cakes are brown and crispy, turn over and cook on the other side briefly, no more than a minute.

Makes about 12 3-inch pancakes (more with tabbouleh added)

18

WHOLE WHEAT BUTTERMILK PANCAKES

Buttermilk used to be the liquid that was left after butter was made from cream. Today, buttermilk is usually a cultured skim milk product, but with the same slightly sour taste of the original. In both forms it is a favored ingredient for making breakfast pancakes. Its tartness counterbalances the taste of all those sweet things we usually put on breakfast pancakes.

1 cup whole wheat flour (all-purpose
flour can be substituted)
1 teaspoon baking powder
1 cup buttermilk
1 egg

1. Mix dry ingredients together in a bowl.

2. Combine buttermilk and egg together and beat well.

3. Combine the two mixtures, and blend briefly.

4. Pour about ¼ cup of batter onto a lightly greased hot pan. Cook until many bubbles appear and top surface becomes set. Turn over and cook the other side until the pancake is done through the center, cooking about 1 minute on each side.

Makes about 8 6-inch pancakes

19

3
THIN BATTERS

Thin batter pancakes do not contain any leavening ingredients or separated egg whites. They are light because they are thin. Most thin batter pancakes are used to enfold other foods. Often they are then reheated in an oven, skillet, or by flambeau. This chapter contains recipes for preparing batters for blintzes, cannelloni, crepes (both entrée and dessert), Hungarian and Oriental pancakes, splatter cakes, and others.

CORN BREAD PANCAKES

*T*his marriage of cornmeal and bread crumbs produces a hearty breakfast pancake that is still thin and light like a crepe. They are particularly good with your favorite syrup (see page 51, Toppings) and with ham or bacon on the side.

½ cup yellow cornmeal
½ cup bread crumbs
1¼ cups milk or water, or mix
2 eggs

1. Combine all ingredients in a bowl and mix well (you can use a blender).

2. Spoon about 2 tablespoons of the batter onto a lightly greased hot pan. Immediately tilt and rotate the pan to spread the batter out thin, round, and even.

3. After the top surface has set (only 1-2 minutes), turn and cook the other side briefly.

Makes about 12 5-inch pancakes

CREPES, FINES HERBES

*D*efinitely an entrée version of this French pancake, fines herbes crepes can be adjusted to suit your taste by the addition or substitution of stocks, herbs, and fillings. One of our favorites is a tarragon and chive crepe, made with chicken stock and filled with diced chicken, Dijon mustard, and melted cheese.

1 cup all-purpose flour
1¼ cups chicken or beef stock, or water
2 eggs, well beaten
1½ teaspoons chopped chives
1½ teaspoons chopped tarragon (you may use a number of different herbs, but the total should equal about 3 teaspoons)

1. Combine all ingredients in a bowl and mix well.

2. Spoon about 2 tablespoons batter onto a lightly greased hot pan. Immediately tilt and rotate the pan to spread the batter out thin, round, and even.

3. After the top surface has set (only a minute or so), turn and cook very briefly on the other side.

4. Remove and set aside to be filled.

Makes about 12 5-inch pancakes

FRENCH CREPES

*F*rench crepes can conjure up different images for different people. For some they are a sweet dessert, doused with cognac and dramatically served, flambeau; for others a delicate, yet savory, seafood dish of lobster or crab. Like most pancakes, French crepes can have a wide range of delightful uses. Sometimes we eat them for breakfast with maple syrup or jam.

1 cup all-purpose flour

3 eggs, well beaten

1¼ cups water, milk, or cream, depending upon how rich you want your crepes (if you use cream, use a little less flour)

1 teaspoon vanilla extract (optional for dessert crepes)

¼ cup sugar (optional for dessert crepes)

1. Combine all ingredients in a bowl and mix well (you can use a blender).

2. Spoon about 2 tablespoons batter onto a lightly greased hot pan. Immediately tilt and rotate the pan to spread the batter out thin, round, and even.

3. After only a minute or so, turn the crepe and cook the other side—but very briefly, unless you are not going to reheat them; in that case, cook for a minute or so, as you would a normal pancake.

Makes about 12 5-inch pancakes

22

HUNGARIAN PALACSINTA

This Hungarian version of the French dessert crepe is sweet and light. Traditionally it is filled and folded, rather than rolled. Palacsinta is often eaten out of hand, or it can be formally served on a plate accompanied by knife and fork. In this case, and as an added delight, fruit brandies may be spooned over the palascinta.

1 cup all-purpose flour
2 teaspoons sugar
2 eggs, well beaten
¾ cup milk
½ teaspoon vanilla extract (other
  flavors optional)
½ cup club soda, from freshly opened
  bottle

1. Combine flour and sugar in a bowl.
2. Combine eggs, milk, and vanilla and mix well.

3. Combine dry and liquid ingredients and mix well. Add club soda and stir briefly.

4. Spoon about 2 tablespoons of batter onto lightly greased hot pan. Immediately turn and tilt the pan to spread the batter out thin, round, and even.

5. Cook until top surface has set. Turn over and cook briefly on the other side. Fill and fold as you would a blintze.

Makes about 12 5-inch pancakes

23

ITALIAN CANNELLONI

*T*hese Italian pancake channels, *cannelloni,* are traditionally served as an entrée with a cream sauce, or use your imagination. The filling doesn't have to be Italian—one of our favorites is feta cheese and spinach.

1¼ cups milk (you can substitute water)
1 cup all-purpose flour
2 eggs

1. Combine milk and flour and mix well.

2. Beat eggs separately and add to the mixture; continue mixing until thoroughly blended (you can use a blender).

3. Spoon about 2 tablespoons onto a lightly greased hot pan. Immediately tilt and rotate the pan to spread the batter out thin, round, and even (add a little more water if the batter does not spread quickly).

4. Remove as soon as the top surface has set. Do not turn the cannelloni over. Remove and set aside for filling and rolling.

Makes about 12 5-inch pancakes

24

LEMON CREPES

*E*ven though we call these crepes, we serve them for breakfast with syrup; as an entrée with seafood, chicken, or vegetable fillings; or as a dessert. This is a very versatile pancake and one of our favorites. The lemon juice and zest balance sweet syrups and sauces, and complement the fillings.

1 cup flour, premix or all-purpose
1 cup water
1 egg
Juice and zest of one large lemon

1. Combine all ingredients in a bowl and mix well with a large spoon. (You can use a blender, but don't blend for more than a few seconds—the lemon zest should not be chopped too fine.)

2. Spoon about 2 tablespoons onto a lightly greased hot pan. Immediately, tilt and rotate the pan to spread the batter out thin, round, and even (add a little more water if the batter does not spread quickly).

3. After only a minute or so, turn the pancake and cook the other side.

Makes about 12 5-inch pancakes

ORIENTAL PANCAKES

*T*hese pancakes can have various finely chopped ingredients added to the batter, or they can be used to enfold other ingredients, like a crepe. In either case these delicate oriental pancakes are refreshingly different and decidedly Eastern.

1 cup all-purpose flour
1¼ cups water
2 eggs, well beaten
1 tablespoon vegetable oil
1 teaspoon soy sauce
½ teaspoon powdered ginger

1. Combine all ingredients in a bowl and mix well.

2. Spoon about 2 tablespoons of batter onto a lightly greased hot pan. Immediately tilt and rotate the pan to spread the batter out thin, round, and even.

3. After the top surface has set (only a minute or more), turn over and cook the other side briefly.

Makes about 12 5-inch pancakes

PASSOVER BLINTZES

*B*lintzes are Jewish pancakes. They are generally filled with cottage cheese, or with lox and onions, or with sweets. Once filled, blintzes are usually folded up rather than rolled; then they can be either baked or fried. Many people use all-purpose flour today, but we think there is something special about using the matzo flour, or cracker meal, that is traditional at Passover.

¾ cup matzo flour, or 4 matzo crackers
*   reduced to meal in a blender/food*
*   processor*
3 eggs, well beaten
1¼ cups freshly opened seltzer water

1. Combine flour and eggs. Add seltzer water and blend quickly.

2. Spoon about 2 tablespoons of batter onto a lightly greased hot pan. Immediately tilt and rotate the pan to spread the batter out thin, round, and even.

3. Remove as soon as the top surface has set; do not turn the blintze over. Set aside for filling and folding. Once the filling has been placed in the center of the uncooked side of the blintze, fold the 4 edges of the blintze toward the center. Turn the blintze over and set aside.

Makes about 12 5-inch blintzes

25

SINGAPORE POH PIAH

*T*his is about as basic a pancake as you can get—it is nothing but flour and water. Rice flour is preferred, but all-purpose flour makes an acceptable substitute. Poh Piah can be filled with a variety of oriental mixtures and then rolled up tightly. In Singapore, Poh Piah is normally fried in deep fat, but we prefer to bake them in an oven. You can take your choice.

*1¼ cups rice flour, or all-purpose flour,
    or a mix of both*
2 scant cups of water

1. Combine flour and water in a bowl and mix well to get all the lumps out (you can use a blender). Let rest for a few minutes.

2. Spoon about 2 tablespoons of the batter onto a lightly greased hot pan. Immediately tilt and rotate the pan to spread the batter out thin, round, and even.

3. Cook for 2–3 minutes, about twice as long as usual. Turn and cook the other side for an equal time.

4. Remove and set aside to be filled.

Makes about 12 5-inch pancakes

26

SOUR CREAM SPLATTER CAKES

*T*hese are very thin pancakes that are fun to make and to eat. Spill the batter into the pans in swirls and circles. Instead of bubbles, holes will appear—making a crispy, lacy pancake around the edges, but soft and creamy in the center. They are different and delicious.

1 cup all-purpose flour, or premix
⅔ cup sour cream
1½ cups water

1. Combine all ingredients in a bowl and mix well.

2. Scoop up the batter with a ¼-cup measure, filling about half full. Spill it quickly onto a lightly greased hot pan, in swirls and circles.

3. When the edges of the pancake begin to get crispy, turn it over and cook briefly on the other side.

Makes about 12 5-inch splatter cakes

TORTILLA CREPES

*U*nlike true tortillas, which are made of dough (see page 46), these pancakes are batter-made. They can be filled and rolled like crepes. The cornmeal gives them a distinctive texture and flavor that goes very well with hearty fillings like ham and cheese, or chopped beef and chili.

1 cup yellow cornmeal
1¼ cups boiling water
2 eggs, well beaten

1. Add cornmeal to the boiling water and mix well, until smooth. Combine with beaten eggs and continue beating.

2. Spoon about 2 tablespoons of the batter onto a lightly greased hot pan. Immediately tilt and rotate the pan to spread the batter out thin, round, and even.

3. After the top surface has set (these pancakes take a little longer than most), remove and set aside.

4. Stir the mixture in the bowl before making the next pancake—cornmeal tends to settle to the bottom. If you are using a blender, give the mixture a brief whirl.

Makes about 12 5-inch tortillas

27

4
THICK BATTERS

Thick batters always contain leavening ingredients—yeast, baking powder, baking soda—plus acid ingredients, or they are made with beaten egg whites. With suitable toppings they can be served as hors d'oeuvres, snacks, or desserts. Some are substantial enough to make a snack or light lunch just as they come out of the pan. This chapter contains recipes for Russian blinis, bannocks, corn pone, crumpets, Korn Eishtars, scones, and others.

AFRICAN BANANA PANCAKES

*I*n many parts of tropical Africa bananas grow plentifully and naturally. They have become one of the staples of the African diet. Sweet corn is also common and is generally known as mealie. Cornmeal is therefore mealie flour. This recipe combines these two basic ingredients into a sweet and spicy pancake that is good for breakfast or dessert. To add a western touch, spoon a little topping (see page 51).

1 cup mashed bananas
½ cup mealie flour (cornmeal)
½ teaspoon ground ginger
½ teaspoon baking powder
1 tablespoon brown sugar
¾ cup water

1. Combine all ingredients in a bowl and mix well (you can use a blender or food processor).

2. Drop about ¼ cup of batter onto a well-greased medium-hot pan. When bubbles appear, turn the pancake over and cook on the other side, cooking about a minute on each side.

Makes about 8 5-inch pancakes

29

BUTTERMILK CORN PONE

*S*outheastern American Indians called bread *pone*. Perhaps this was a derivation of the Spanish word for bread, *pan*. In any case the word *pone* survived throughout the South to describe simple, quick-rising breads, often pan-fried. This more elegant version is delicious with applesauce or other fruit toppings (see page 52).

1 cup cornmeal
1 teaspoon baking powder
1 cup buttermilk

1. Mix cornmeal and baking powder together in a bowl. Add buttermilk and stir until well blended.

2. Pour about ¼ cup of batter onto a lightly greased hot pan. Cook until many bubbles appear and top surface becomes set. Turn over and cook the other side until the pancake is done through the center, cooking about a minute on each side.

Makes about 8 5-inch pancakes

BRITISH BANNOCKS

*T*here are as many ways to make bannocks as there are legends about them. According to Druid belief, you must always beat your bannock batter from east to west, the way the sun goes, to make them as good as they should be. King Alfred the Great is supposed to have committed the unpardonable sin of burning the bannocks in the shack of a peasant woman when he was escaping in disguise from the Danish army—she nearly turned him out until he told her who he was. Bannocks can be made either plain or filled with nuts and fruits (see page 53, Add-Ins).

½ cup all-purpose flour
½ cup rolled oats, (breakfast oatmeal,
    either quick or regular)
1 teaspoon baking powder
1 tablespoon granulated sugar
¼ teaspoon cinnamon
2 eggs
1 cup milk
½ cup dried currants, raisins, chopped
    nuts, or diced fruit (optional)

30

1. Combine dry ingredients and mix well in a bowl.

2. Combine eggs and milk and beat to a froth, then add to the dry ingredients. Add fruit or nuts, if desired, and mix well.

3. Spoon about 2 tablespoons of batter onto a lightly greased hot pan. When many bubbles appear on the top surface, turn and cook on the other side until done through the center.

Makes about 12 3-inch bannocks

CHIPS AND GRITS

*D*espite the incongruous combination of chocolate chips and hominy grits, these turn out to be a deliciously different dessert pancake. With a little Cointreau spooned over them they can turn grits into a gourmet delight. (See page 51, Toppings, for other serving suggestions.)

1 cup hominy grits (we prefer the dried, prepared variety)
¼ cup all-purpose flour
½ cup milk
½ cup chocolate chips (you can use more if you like)
2 eggs, separated

1. Cook hominy grits at least 5 minutes—they should not be gritty.

2. Mix all ingredients except the egg whites in a bowl.

3. Beat egg whites until stiff, then fold into the mixture.

4. Drop about ¼ cup of batter onto a well-greased hot pan. Cook about a minute, then turn over and cook the other side.

5. Remove and serve at once, either by themselves or with topping of your choice.

Makes about 8 5-inch pancakes

HOE CAKES OR JOHNNY CAKES

*T*hese were originally called *journey cakes* because they were the staple food of settlers moving west during the nineteenth century. Since they were often cooked over an open fire on the greased surface of a flat hoe blade, they are also called *hoe cakes*. This is basic, hearty pioneer fare. Topped with molasses, honey, jam, or maple syrup, it is also delicious.

1 cup yellow cornmeal
1½ cups boiling water

1. Slowly add cornmeal to the boiling water, stirring constantly to avoid lumps. Remove from heat and continue stirring until mixture is smooth.

2. Pour ¼ cup of batter onto a well-greased hot pan. Cook for 2–3 minutes on each side, or until pancake is cooked through.

Makes about 8 5-inch hoe cakes

CRANBERRY PUFF CAKES

Without a doubt, this is our family's favorite breakfast pancake. The combination of tart cranberries and sweet syrup is an irresistible taste sensation. The cakes are so light and airy, they disappear as fast as you can make them. Enjoy them from fall through winter when fresh cranberries are plentiful.

½ cup all-purpose flour
½ cup whole wheat flour
¼ cup Wheatina or yellow cornmeal
1½ cups water
3 eggs, separated
1 cup, or more, fresh cranberries

1. Mix flours, Wheatina or cornmeal, water, and egg yolks in a bowl.

2. Beat the egg whites until stiff and fold into mixture.

3. Add cranberries and fold them into mixture.

4. Drop about ⅓ cup of the mixture onto a well-greased hot pan. Cook about a minute and a half, or until edges become crispy. Turn over and cook the other side.

Note: 1¼ cups all-purpose flour may be substituted for the first 3 ingredients.

Makes about 12 5-inch puff cakes

32

IRISH BOXTY

*B*oxty is the traditional potato pancake of Ireland, particularly in the northern counties. "Boxty on the griddle, boxty in the pan. If ye can't make boxty, ye'll never get a man."—The verse is pretty much the same throughout Ireland, but the recipes for boxty vary considerably. Some call for grated raw potatoes, some call for cooked mashed potatoes, and some for a mixture of both. This recipe gives you the choice—try boxty both ways.

*¾ cup raw potato, grated, or mashed
    potato (leftovers are fine)*
½ cup all-purpose flour
1 teaspoon baking powder
*¼–½ cup milk (you will need less milk
    with the grated potatoes)*
1 egg, beaten

1. Combine potato, flour, baking powder, and enough milk to make a thick batter. Mix well.

2. Add the well-beaten egg and continue mixing.

3. Spoon about 2 tablespoons of batter onto a well-greased medium-hot pan. Cook until pancake is brown and crispy around the edges, then turn over and cook on the other side. Boxty cooks slower than most pancakes; be careful to cook through.

Makes about 12 3-inch boxty

33

KORN EISHTARS

*T*his is a Pennsylvania Dutch recipe for something that doesn't look or taste much like fried oysters, but is called *korn eishtars* (corn oysters). The original recipe calls for slitting the rows of kernels on uncooked ears of fresh corn, then squeezing out the meaty insides of each kernel with the back edge of a knife. We started using hominy grits, basically the same ingredient, when fresh corn was unavailable. Now we use hominy grits all the time. Despite their strange name and common ingredients, these are light and delightful little cakes—to serve on the side instead of potatoes, or as dessert (see page 31, Chips and Grits).

*1 cup hominy grits (we prefer the
    dried, prepared variety)*
¼ cup whole wheat flour
½ cup water
2 eggs, separated

1. Cook hominy grits at least 5 minutes—they should not be gritty.

2. Mix all ingredients except the egg whites in a bowl.

3. Beat egg whites until they are stiff, then fold into the mixture.

4. Drop about a tablespoon of batter onto a well-greased hot pan. Cook about a minute and then turn pancakes over and cook about a minute on the other side. The "oysters" should be golden brown on both sides.

Makes about 16 2-inch eishtars

34

POLENTA PANCAKES

*P*olenta is an Italian version of American cornmeal mush. It is the basis for a whole spectrum of dishes, including pancakes. These make a simple, hearty entrée that can be served with a cream sauce, a tomato sauce, or melted butter.

½ cup yellow cornmeal
1½ cups boiling water
1 egg, well beaten
¾ cup grated Parmesan or Romano
    cheese
¼ cup chopped oregano or basil

1. Slowly add cornmeal to the boiling water, stirring constantly to avoid lumps. Remove from heat and continue stirring until mixture is smooth. Set aside to cool.

2. Add remaining ingredients and mix well.

3. Spoon about 2 tablespoons of batter onto a lightly greased hot pan. Cook for 2–3 minutes on each side, or until the pancake is cooked through.

Makes about 12 3-inch pancakes

35

RUSSIAN BLINIS

*B*linis are traditionally served during the Lenten season, but they are just as delicious year-round. They are normally made with buckwheat flour and a yeast-rising batter. Since buckwheat flour is often hard to find and yeast-rising batters are time-consuming, we have given you a recipe that uses the standard buckwheat mix which has a quick-rising leavening agent in the mix. Blinis are usually served with caviar and sour cream, with chopped eggs and cottage cheese, or with chopped parsley and onion (see page 51, Toppings).

1 cup buckwheat pancake mix
1 cup milk or water
1 tablespoon vegetable oil
2 eggs, separated

1. Combine all ingredients but the egg whites in a bowl, and mix well.

2. Beat the egg whites until they form stiff peaks, then fold into the batter.

3. Spoon one generous tablespoon of batter onto a lightly greased hot pan, spreading the top out flat as you do so. Cook blini for about one minute, or until the edges begin to crisp up, then turn and cook the other side until it is cooked through.

Makes about 16 2-inch blinis

POLISH POTATO PANCAKES

With a name like *Zabriskie,* we should find these our favorite pancakes—and we do. Light and flavorful, they can accompany a meat dish, or stand by themselves for a nutritious luncheon with applesauce on the side.

1 medium potato, cubed
1 tablespoon diced onion
2 tablespoons sour cream
1 egg, separated
½ teaspoon chopped parsley
½ teaspoon chopped dill weed
¼ cup whole wheat flour

1. Place potato, onion, sour cream, and egg yolk in a blender or food processor, and reduce to a thick sauce. Pour into a bowl.

2. Add herbs and flour and mix well.

3. Beat egg white in a small bowl until it forms stiff peaks, then fold into the mixture.

4. Spoon about 2 tablespoons of batter onto a well-greased medium-hot pan. When edges of pancake begin to crisp up, turn over and cook on the other side, cooking a little more than a minute on each side.

Makes about 12 3-inch pancakes

36

SWEET AND SOUR CAKES

*T*his is an unusual dessert pancake that offers opposing tastes and textures, combining bits of sweet in a sour cream base. We like them particularly with chocolate chips in the batter, but try them with your favorite candied chip or diced candied fruit. To gild the lily a little, spoon some after-dinner liqueur over the pancakes—white crème de menthe goes especially well with chocolate chips (see page 51, Toppings).

¾ cup all-purpose flour
⅓ cup sour cream
⅓ cup water
½ cup chocolate chips, or other sweet
    bits of your choice
2 eggs, separated

1. Combine flour, sour cream, water, sweet bits, and egg yolks in a bowl and mix well.

2. Beat egg whites until they form stiff peaks, then fold into the mixture.

3. Spoon about 2 tablespoons of batter onto a lightly greased hot pan. Cook for a little over a minute on each side, or until top and bottom are a crispy brown.

Makes about 12 3-inch pancakes

37

QUICK-RISING CRUMPETS

*C*rumpets are the light, round cakes that so often accompany tea in England. They are also served at breakfast. They can be baked or pan fried, and are usually made with a yeast-rising batter. The less common quick-rising version is given here, since few of us have the time or the inclination to produce yeast-rising pancakes. If you want truly round crumpets, cut both ends out of a tuna or similar 6½-ounce can and cook the crumpet inside the can.

1 cup all-purpose flour
½ teaspoon baking powder
1 tablespoon granulated sugar
1 tablespoon vegetable oil
1 cup milk
1 egg, separated

1. Combine dry ingredients in a bowl.
2. Combine oil, milk, and egg yolk and beat well, then add to the dry ingredients and mix well.

3. Beat egg white until it makes stiff peaks, then fold into the mixture.
4. Drop about 2 tablespoons of batter onto a lightly greased hot pan. (If you use can forms, drop inside the cans.) When the crumpets have set on the top side, turn over and cook on the other side. (Slip out of the cans to cook the other side.)

Makes about 12 3-inch crumpets

SCOTCH DROP SCONES

Scones are the traditional small breads of Scotland. Served for breakfast or at teatime, they are usually baked. However, drop scones, made from batter and pan-fried, are also popular. The Scots are big oat eaters. Oats find their way into many recipes, including haggis, the famous and unusual dish made from the stomach, liver, and heart of a sheep, plus oats. The rolled oats in this recipe add a north country, hearty quality to these Scotch pancakes.

1½ cups all-purpose flour
*½ cup rolled oats (breakfast oatmeal,
    either quick or regular)*
1 teaspoon baking powder
2 tablespoons granulated sugar
1 egg
1 cup milk

1. Combine dry ingredients in a bowl and mix well.

2. Combine egg and milk and beat to a froth, then add to the dry ingredients and mix well.

3. Spoon 2 tablespoons of batter onto a lightly greased hot pan. When many bubbles appear on the top surface, turn and cook on the other side; it should take about a minute on each side.

4. Serve immediately with butter and jam.

*Makes about 24 3-inch scones (a double
    recipe)*

39

5

BAKED PANCAKES
AND
DOUGH PANCAKES

In this chapter you will find recipes for a few pancakes that, while they do not follow normal pancake procedures, are well worth making.

The first group of pancakes are all made with a batter, but are baked in an oven instead of being cooked over a fire. These recipes include Dutch Baby, Dixie Baby, and a quick quiche with a number of variations.

The second group are made from dough that is flattened and rolled out to produce a thin disc—which is then pan-fried like a conventional pancake. These recipes include Indian chappaties, Mexican tortillas, Irish fadge, and mandarin pancakes.

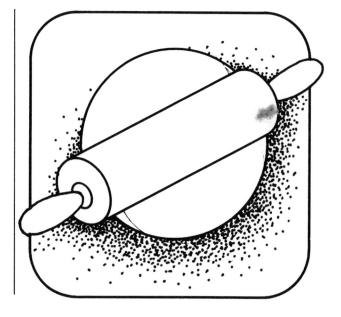

DUTCH BABY

We don't know how this rather dramatic dish got its name and neither does our artist friend who gave us the recipe. What it is, however, is a giant flat-topped popover. What it does is provide you with an almost effortless breakfast for four or more. The blender and oven do all the work for you. Minding a Dutch Baby is a breeze.

⅓ stick margarine or butter
1 cup all-purpose flour
1 cup milk
4 eggs

1. Preheat oven to 450°F.

2. When oven is hot, put margarine in a 10-inch all-metal skillet and place in oven.

3. When margarine has melted and begins to bubble, place all remaining ingredients in a blender and blend thoroughly at high speed, about a minute.

4. Open the oven just enough to pour the batter quickly into the skillet. Close and bake for about 20 minutes, or until the "Baby" has popped up over the edge of the pan and is a delicious golden brown. Serve at once with a topping of your choice.

Makes 1 10-inch pancake

41

DIXIE BABY

*T*his is a Southern version of the Dutch Baby—very different in taste, but just as quick and easy to prepare.

⅓ *stick margarine or butter*
½ *cup cornmeal*
½ *cup whole wheat flour*
4 eggs
1 cup milk
¼ *cup molasses*

1. Preheat oven to 450°F.

2. When oven is hot, put margarine in a 10-inch all-metal skillet and place in oven.

3. When margarine has melted and begins to bubble, place all remaining ingredients in a blender and blend thoroughly at high speed, about a minute.

4. Open the oven just enough to pour the batter quickly into the skillet. Close and bake for about 20 minutes, or until the "Baby" has popped up over the edge of the pan and is a delicious golden brown. Serve at once with a topping of your choice.

Makes 1 10-inch puffed-up pancake

42

QUICK QUICHE

This very useful dish is a cross between a restrained Dutch Baby, an enlarged bread crumb pancake, and the classic French quiche. What it does is provide you with a quick and easy luncheon for four. The recipe given here is only one suggestion; the possibilities are endless. See page 53, Add-Ins, or use your imagination. (For this recipe the amount of add-ins should be doubled.)

⅓ stick margarine or butter
⅔ cup all-purpose flour
⅓ cup bread crumbs
1 cup milk
4 eggs
2 tablespoons Dijon mustard
½ cup diced ham
½ cup diced Swiss cheese

1. Preheat oven to 450°F.

2. When oven is hot, put margarine in a 10-inch all-metal skillet and place in oven.

3. When margarine has melted and begins to bubble, place all remaining ingredients except ham and cheese in the blender. Blend thoroughly at high speed, about a minute. Add the ham and cheese and mix thoroughly with a spoon (*not* the blender).

4. Open the oven just enough to pour the batter quickly into the skillet. Close and bake for about 10–15 minutes, until the quiche has set.

Serves 4–6

43

QUICK QUICHE VARIATIONS

*I*n the following recipes the basic batter mix remains the same—⅓ stick margarine or butter, ⅔ cup all-purpose flour, ⅓ cup bread crumbs, 1 cup milk, and 4 eggs; it is the add-ins that vary. Directions for making all variations are the same as for the previous recipe.

FETA CHEESE AND SPINACH

Basic batter
2 tablespoons Dijon mustard
½ cup feta cheese, crumbled
½ cup chopped frozen spinach,
*   defrosted*
¼ cup plain yogurt

CHICKEN AND CHEDDAR

Basic batter
2 tablespoons Dijon mustard
½ cup cooked chicken, cubed
½ cup cheddar cheese, cubed
½ tablespoon dill weed, fresh or dried

ITALIAN SAUSAGE

Basic batter
¼ cup tomato sauce
½ teaspoon garlic, fresh chopped, or
*   garlic powder*
½ tablespoon dried oregano
½ cup sweet or hot Italian sausage,
*   well cooked and diced*
½ cup mozzarella cheese, shredded

INDIAN CHAPPATIES

*C*happaties are both food and eating utensil. Since much of the Indian cuisine consists of a variety of foods prepared in rich sauces, curries, and pilaus, and since most Indian families see no need for silverware, a piece of chappati is used to scoop up the food and convey it to the mouth. Next time you serve a curry dish, try chappaties. They are easier to use than chopsticks, there will be no silverware to wash, and they are good to eat. You can also use them as you would a crepe.

1½ cups whole wheat flour
¾ cup water (approximate)

1. In a bowl, slowly add the water to the flour until you produce a ball of dough that is cohesive and not sticky. Knead the ball briefly with your fingers.

2. Nip off a piece of dough about the size of a small egg, and roll it into a ball.

3. With a rolling pin, roll out the ball on a floured surface into a flat disc no more than ⅛ inch thick.

4. Cook the chappati on a lightly greased hot pan for about a minute on each side. Do not overcook, or the chappati will become stiff and difficult to use.

Makes about 8 5-inch chappaties

45

IRISH FADGE

*T*hese potato dough cakes are most common in the northern part of Ireland. They are an efficient way to use up leftover mashed potatoes and make a delicious, hearty breakfast served with eggs and bacon or ham.

1½ cups mashed potatoes
½ cup all-purpose flour
1 tablespoon vegetable oil

1. Combine all ingredients in a bowl. Knead well with your fingers to produce a homogenous dough.

2. Nip off small egg-sized pieces of dough; roll them into balls and then squash them into round discs about ½ inch thick.

3. Cook the fadge on a well-greased medium-hot pan until the edges are brown and crispy, then turn over and cook the other side.

Makes about 8 5-inch fadges

MEXICAN TORTILLAS

Without a tortilla press, making these versatile Mexican pancakes can be difficult and discouraging. However, the Mexicans themselves made tortillas for centuries before the metal press was invented, so we set out to make historic tortillas. They will not be as round and perfect as the ones you can buy from the store, but they will be just as good—maybe better—and they will be yours. *Masa Harina*, the precooked corn flour, is an absolute necessity. You can find it at stores that specialize in Hispanic foods.

1 cup Masa Harina
1 cup hot water (more or less)
Waxed paper for rolling out the tortillas

1. Add water slowly to the *Masa Harina* in a bowl. Knead the dough with your fingers. Keep adding water and kneading the dough until you produce a ball of dough that is not sticky and that holds together well.

2. Pinch off a small egg-sized piece of dough. Roll it into a ball and then, using a flat surface, roll it into a cylinder with the palm of your hand.

3. Place the cylinder of dough between two sheets of wax paper and roll it out with a rolling pin into an approximate circle.

4. Peel the tortilla off the wax paper and cook on a very lightly greased hot pan for a minute or more until the bottom is flecked with brown spots. Turn over and cook the other side.

Makes about 8 5-inch tortillas

46

MANDARIN PANCAKES

*M*andarin means *aristocrat* in Chinese. Mandarin cooking, centered in Peking, is the traditional gourmet cuisine of China. With mandarin pancakes, the Chinese approach the idea of thin from a completely different point of view. The pancakes are made from dough, not batter. Two pancakes are rolled out together and then pulled apart, to make the thinnest pancake possible. These pancakes can be used to hold food for eating, like Mu Shu Pork, or they can be filled and rolled like crepes.

1 cup all-purpose flour
½ teaspoon soy oil or other vegetable oil
½ cup boiling water
Oil for brushing

1. Combine flour and ½ teaspoon oil, then add half the water. Blend the mixture with a spoon. Gradually add more water until a dough ball is made that does not stick to your fingers. Knead the dough with your fingers. If you have put too much water in, add a little more flour. Once the dough ball is firm and not sticky, let it rest for 10–15 minutes.

2. Pinch off pieces of dough and roll them up into walnut-sized balls. On a smooth floured surface, push the balls into round discs. Separate half the discs, and oil the top surface of these. Place the other discs on top and roll out the two together as thin as possible.

3. Place one pair of pancakes on a hot, ungreased pan. After about one minute the top surface will bubble up. Turn the pair of pancakes over and cook for about a minute on the other side. Remove and set aside.

4. When the pancakes have cooled, gently pull the pair apart. You will have two very thin, flexible pancakes to use as you wish.

Makes about 8 5-inch pancakes

47

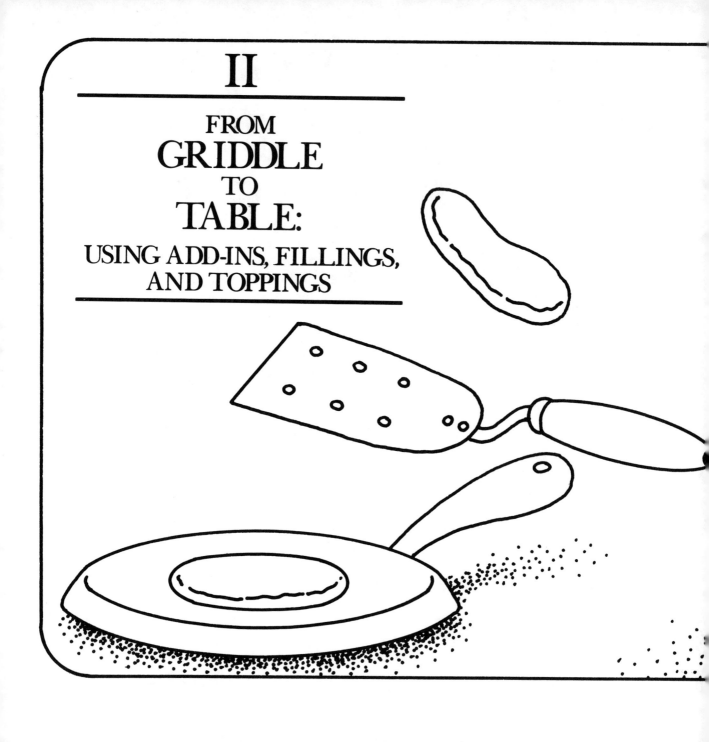

II

FROM
GRIDDLE
TO
TABLE:
USING ADD-INS, FILLINGS, AND TOPPINGS

6
BREAKFAST

The great majority of the people in the world think of pancakes as a handy way to enfold other foods to eat for lunch, dinner, or dessert. They do not normally think of starting off their day with them. The great majority of Americans, however, when they think of pancakes, think of breakfast. They think of a stack of pancakes topped with pools of melted butter and dripping with maple syrup. More likely, the stack of pancakes will be topped by pools of melted margarine and dripping in syrup that is 2 percent maple. Americans also tend to think of pancakes as a special breakfast to be served only on weekends when some member of the family will take the time to make them. Actually, pancakes take only a few minutes to prepare—even starting from scratch—and the cooking process should not take more than a minute or two per batch. If you can allow ten minutes to fix breakfast, you can fix a pancake breakfast any day of the week. They are especially good in cool weather when the aroma of hot cakes on the stove and the sight of hot cakes on the table is irresistible.

All of the normal and thin batters will make delicious breakfast pancakes. All of the thick batters may be served for breakfast, too, and they will be quite a change from what most Americans are used to thinking of as pancakes. All of these will go very well with butter and syrup, but there are lots of other toppings you can use—and a number of add-ins you can stir into the batter to produce nutritious new tastes and textures. In this chapter you will find ways to make pancake breakfasts so different and delicious—and so easy to prepare—that you might want to try them every day of the week.

TOPPINGS

Syrups

The almost universal syrup to be found on top of American breakfast pancakes is called "maple syrup" by most of us. Pure maple syrup is a true American culinary creation—the American Indians were tapping maple trees and boiling down syrup long before the first colonists arrived. However, pure maple syrup is a very special and expensive treat. Most commercial brands are composed of artificially flavored corn syrup; there is very little in them that ever saw a maple tree.

Here are some suggested syrups, both ready-made and easy to make, for your breakfast pancakes.

- **Pure Maple Syrup**—rich, thick, flavorful, and delicious.

- **Maple-Flavored Syrup**—contains a large proportion of pure maple syrup stretched with less expensive syrups, usually from corn.

- **Brand-Name Syrups**—these usually contain about 2 percent pure maple syrup; the rest is artificially flavored and colored corn syrup.

- **Honey**—the most common sweetener in the world until recently, when commercial sugar production became possible. There are many varieties of honey depending upon the source of the nectar; all are thick, heavy, and very sweet.

- **Lemon Honey**—an easy-to-make syrup—less sweet, less thick, and less heavy than honey. The syrup is made by combining 1/3 to 1/2 cup lemon juice to a cup of honey. Make sure the liquids are well mixed. Lemon honey will keep for a few weeks in the refrigerator.

- **Molasses**—a by-product of commercial sugar manufacture, it is sold in three grades—light, dark, and blackstrap—depending upon whether it comes from the first, second, or third step in the sugar-making process. Unless you are a confirmed molasses lover, the light variety is probably the best for a pancake syrup.

51

- **Corn Syrup**—made from the glucose that makes sweet corn sweet, it is produced in two varieties—light and dark. Again we suggest using the lighter syrup, since it is clear and has very little flavor. You can enhance this syrup with spices like powdered cinnamon or ginger, or with flavored extracts like vanilla, lemon, almond, or others. In effect, you can make your own favorite-flavored pancake syrup. Just be sure that the flavorings and syrup base are well mixed.

- **Simple Syrup**—an easy to make, do-it-yourself syrup that yields about 3 cups of syrup. Simply boil 2 cups of water with 1–1½ cups of sugar until the sugar is completely dissolved. Continue boiling until the syrup is of the pouring consistency that pleases you. Add any of the above flavorings that you wish, mix well, and pour with pride: You made your own pancake syrup.

Fruits

A healthful breakfast should contain the vitamins and minerals that fruits generally provide, especially vitamin C. Fruits, plus the carbohydrates and proteins that most pancake recipes provide, make a nutritionally balanced breakfast as well. Fruits in their various forms can provide a whole spectrum of delicious toppings for your breakfast pancakes. Here are some suggested ways to use fruits for this purpose.

- **Jam**—a favorite topping in Europe, where flavored syrups in general, and maple syrup in particular, are not common items on supermarket shelves. Jams of all kinds, spread as thick or as thin as you wish, make marvelous pancake toppings. Jam stays where it's put. It doesn't run off the pancake to form a gooey pool that is likely to remain after all the pancakes have been eaten. Jam can be spread on a pancake and the pancake rolled up and eaten out of hand. Try *that* with a syrup and see what happens.

- **Sliced Strawberries with Powdered Sugar**—an elegant topping for very special breakfasts.

- **Smashed Berries**—an easy-to-make topping for all kinds of berries when they are very ripe. Place the berries—strawberries, raspberries, blackberries, blueberries, or any other soft, ripe berries—in a bowl. Smash them up with a fork to form a homogenous mass. Add sugar to your taste and a little water to make the mixture spreadable. Smashed berry toppings should be used the same day they are prepared. They can be kept a day or two in the refrigerator, but they are best fresh.

- **Puree of Fruit**—this is an almost-anything-will-work kind of topping that you can make in your blender or food processor. Place one or two cups of berries or diced fruit in a blender or food processor. Blend for only a second or two. Check for consistency and sweetness of the puree. Add water or sugar, or both, to suit your taste, then blend briefly again. The puree can be used alone as a topping—or it can be enhanced with a second variety of small berry (like blueberries) or diced firm fruit (like apples or pineapples). A little powdered sugar sprinkled on top adds a touch of elegance. A puree of apricots, enhanced with whole cranberries, is one of our favorites.

- **Pineapple Ring Filled with Fruit Puree**—Instead of putting small fruits in the puree, put the puree in the center of a large fruit. Tinned pineapple rings filled with raspberry puree makes a great color, taste, and texture combination.

- **Cantaloupe Ring with Green Grapes**—This is a sophisticated, all-fresh, all-natural topping that turns a common pancake breakfast into a special occasion.

ADD-INS

Most of us tend to think that a pancake is a pancake is a pancake—a batter-based breakfast food cooked on a griddle. But in many parts of the world people add all sorts of things to their batters. This makes a pancake that is more delicious, more nutritious, and much more interesting. Adding in other ingredients opens up a whole spectrum of new possibilities for breakfast pancakes. Of course, blueberry pancakes have been a favorite for a long time, but there are other things besides blueberries that you can put in a pancake. Here are some of our suggestions. These will work well in any of our normal or thick batter pancakes.

- **Berries**—Any small berry will add zest to any pancake. Try adding half a cup of currants, cranberries, tiny fraise des bois (wild strawberries), or blueberries to your pancake batter.

- **Diced Fruits**—Any firm fruit (like an apple, pineapple, or even a peach) diced into small bits, will add flavor, texture, and nutrition to your pancake batter.

53

- **Dried Fruits**—Dried currants or raisins are naturals for batter add-ins. Larger dried fruits, like apples and prunes, can be cut into small bits and added to your batter.

- **Cereals**—A number of prepared cereals, like Grape Nuts or rolled oats or granola chunks broken into bits, will add nutrition and texture to your batter.

- **Seeds and Nuts**—A whole variety of seeds and chopped nuts can be added to pancake batters. Sesame seeds (also called bennes), chopped walnuts, chopped almonds—almost any small seed or chopped nut—will add interest, taste, and texture to your batter.

- **Combinations**—With batter add-ins there is no need to stay with only one ingredient. Combine chopped nuts with dried fruits or fresh fruits. Mix it up with sesame seeds, dried apple bits, and blueberries. You can hardly go wrong—all the combinations will be both nutritious and delicious. One point to remember is to keep the add-ins between ½ and ¾ cup in total amount for the standard recipe.

54

7
HORS d'OEUVRES

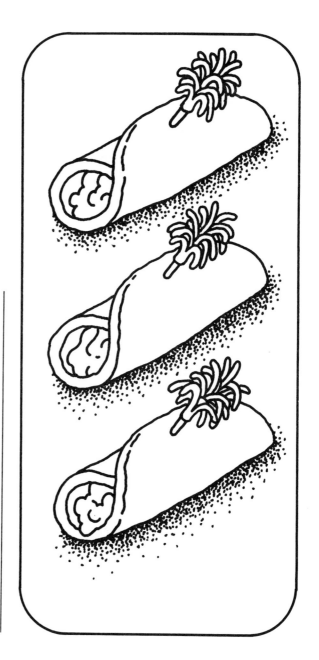

The perfect hors d'oeuvre would be a finger food that was bite-sized, that was absolutely delicious, that none of your guests had ever tasted before, and that did not drip, spill, or crumble on the way from platter to mouth. From *your* point of view, these little delicacies should also be simple to prepare in a short period of time.

One successful and satisfying approach is this: savory foods rolled up in thin pancakes, prepared with ingredients that will stay together. Or you can go the blini route, and prepare small silver dollar–sized firm pancakes that can support a variety of exotic toppings. Or, as a third alternative, you can incorporate the savory ingredients directly in the batter. In this chapter you will find a number of recipes in all three categories.

OKONOMIYAKI

*I*t was this Japanese pancake, served to us by friends, that first opened up the possibilities of adding a variety of ingredients to a basic pancake batter and producing a whole new spectrum of exciting dishes. A few suggested recipes follow, but almost any tasteful combination will work if the add-ins are chopped into small bits. Although listed here as hors d'oeuvres, these pancakes can serve equally well as a light lunch or even a dinner entrée.

We suggest using the batter of one of the following pancakes:

- **Oriental Pancakes** (see page 25)

- **Sour Cream Cakes** (see page 18)

- **Bits and Brew Cakes**, but leave out the bits (see page 13)

½ cup cooked shrimp, chopped (tinned baby shrimp may be used)
⅓ cup fresh bean sprouts or other sprouts of your choice
1 tablespoon fresh scallion, chopped

1 tablespoon fresh ginger, chopped (or powdered ginger)
One of the above-suggested pancake batters, to make 8 pancakes

1. Combine all add-in ingredients with the pancake batter, and mix well before cooking. Once the add-ins are in the batter, *do not* use a blender or food processor.
2. Follow cooking directions for the pancake batter of your choice.
Serves 4

OKONOMIYAKI INTERNATIONAL VARIATIONS

Why not try a few other fillings that we have enjoyed as add-ins for hors d'oeuvre pancakes? We often make them small—silver dollar size—roll them up, and hold them with a toothpick. They then become easy-to-manage, bite-sized finger food. For a midwestern American version, see page 13, Bits and Brew Cakes.

LEBANESE TABBOULEH

1 cup bulgur wheat
½ cup peeled cucumber, diced
¼ cup lemon juice
1 teaspoon fresh minced garlic or garlic
    powder
1 teaspoon dried mint
Pancake batter (Oriental, Sour Cream,
    or Bits and Brew minus bits)

1. In a bowl, cover the bulgur wheat with hot water and let stand for 30 minutes. The water will be absorbed.

2. Combine with the other add-in ingredients and toss together to mix well. Then add to the batter and mix again before cooking. Follow cooking directions for the batter of your choice.

EGYPTIAN FALAFEL

¾ cup beef or chicken stock
1 cup bulgur wheat
¼ cup sesame seeds
¼ cup black olives, pitted and chopped
¼ cup red and/or green peppers,
    chopped
1 tablespoon chili powder
Pancake batter (Oriental, Sour Cream,
    or Bits and Brew minus bits)

1. Heat the beef stock in a saucepan and pour over the bulgur wheat. Let stand for 30 minutes; the liquid will be absorbed.

2. Combine with the other add-in ingredients and toss together to mix well. Then add to batter and mix again before cooking. Follow cooking directions for the batter of your choice.

57

NEW ENGLAND CLAMS

1 cup chopped clams, tinned or fresh
½ cup plain yogurt
¼ cup chopped chives
⅛ cup fresh lemon juice
Freshly ground black pepper to taste

Pancake batter (Oriental, Sour Cream, or Bits and Brew minus bits)

Combine all add-in ingredients with the batter and mix well before cooking. Follow cooking directions for the batter of your choice.

DOLMAS
(STUFFED GRAPE LEAVES)

This traditional Greek dish is delicious, but a bit messy as finger food. Wrapping in a pancake solves that problem. In this recipe you prepare your own filling. Don't worry about tucking in the ends of the grape leaves as neatly as those you find in restaurants—the pancake helps keep the dolmas together. Or, if you wish, you can use prepared dolmas; they are available fresh or canned.

½ cup cooked rice
3 tablespoons plain yogurt
1 tablespoon finely chopped fresh dill
   (or 1 teaspoon dried dill)
¼ cup dried currants
1 tablespoon pine nuts (optional)
Fresh lemon juice to taste
12 grape leaves (available canned at
   most supermarkets)
12 thin Lemon Crepe Pancakes, about
   3 inches in diameter (see page 24)

1. Combine first six ingredients to make the filling.

2. Rinse and drain grape leaves and place on pancakes.

3. Place 1 tablespoon of filling on each grape leaf. Roll up and tuck in ends, then roll up in pancake and hold with toothpick.

4. Serve cold, or place in 350°F. oven for 10 minutes or until heated through.

Makes 12 dolmas

58

LIPTAUER KASE

*T*his Hungarian dish probably never saw a pancake until we put them together. Wrapped up in this version, it makes a savory finger food for cocktail snacking.

½ cup cottage cheese
½ cup softened butter or margarine
½ teaspoon caraway seed
½ teaspoon anchovy paste
1 teaspoon capers
1 teaspoon Dijon mustard
1 tablespoon scallions or chives, chopped fine

½ cup cooked red potatoes, cubed
12 thin pancakes, crepes, or other 5-inch pancakes

1. Combine all filling ingredients and mix well.
2. Fill and roll pancakes. Serve at room temperature.
Makes 12 pieces

POTATO WITH SOUR CREAM AND CAPERS

59

1 cup potatoes, mashed, or baked and peeled
⅓ cup sour cream
2 tablespoons capers
¼ cup melted butter or margarine
1 tablespoon chopped chives
12 thin crepe pancakes, about 3 inches in diameter (see page 22)

1. Combine all of the filling ingredients. Fill and roll pancakes.
2. Hold each pancake together with a toothpick and serve warm.
Makes 12 pieces

PROSCIUTTO AND HONEYDEW

16 slices prosciutto
8 thin Lemon Crepe Pancakes, about 5
    inches in diameter (see page 24)
½ honeydew melon, sliced
4 limes (2 for their juice, 2 for garnish)

1. Place 2 slices of prosciutto on each crepe. Place 2-3 slices honeydew on prosciutto. Squeeze lime juice to taste.
2. Roll up pancakes; garnish with lime slices. Serve at room temperature.

Makes 8 pieces

SEVICHE

*T*his marinated fish dish from Mexico is a delightfully different taste treat served conventionally with bowl and fork. Wrapped in a light little pancake, it makes a delicious cocktail finger food.

Marinade
½ cup fresh lime juice
¼ cup olive oil
2 tablespoons green pepper, chopped
2 tablespoons scallions, chopped
¼ cup green chilies, chopped
½ cup canned tomatoes, drained and
    chopped
½ teaspoon oregano

1 pound firm-fleshed fish or scallops,
    or mixture, chopped

24 thin Lemon Crepe Pancakes, about
    3 inches in diameter (see page 24)

1. Combine marinade ingredients and mix well. Add fish and refrigerate overnight.
2. Drain mixture in a colander.
3. Place 1 tablespoon of the mixture in the center of each pancake. Roll up and hold in place with a toothpick.

Makes 24 pieces

SMOKED OYSTERS WITH BACON

*6 slices bacon, almost cooked and cut
   in half*
*12 thin, crepe-type pancakes, about 3
   inches in diameter*
1 tin smoked oysters (12 oysters)

1. Preheat oven to 425°F.
2. Place 1 half slice of bacon on each pancake. Place 1 oyster on each piece of bacon. Roll up and hold with toothpick.
3. Place seam side down in a buttered dish and bake about 7–10 minutes, or until bacon is crisp.

Makes 12 pieces

BLINTZES WITH LOX
AND ONIONS

Blintzes make about as perfect an hors d'oeuvre package as can be designed. By folding the four corners of the pancake toward the center and then cooking it, you make a very secure finger food container. Of course, other thin pancakes can be folded in this manner too (see page 23, Hungarian Palacsinta).

¼ pound lox, sliced thin and diced
¼ cup red onion, chopped fine
⅛ cup lemon juice
½ cup sour cream
*8 blintzes or other thin pancakes, about
   5 inches in diameter*

1. Combine all filling ingredients in a bowl and mix well.

2. Place about 2 tablespoons of filling in the center of each blintze. Fold the 4 edges of the blintze toward the center and then turn over on the seam side.

3. Place all the blintzes seam side down in a well-buttered hot frying pan. Sauté until golden brown; turn over and cook the other side until heated through.

Makes 8 pieces

61

SPICED HAM AND EGG

1 cup scrambled or hard-boiled eggs,
    chopped fine
¼ cup mayonnaise, preferably
    homemade (see page 95)
1 tablespoon Dijon mustard
2 tablespoons finely chopped ham
2 tablespoons fresh parsley
Freshly ground pepper to taste

24 thin crepe-type pancakes, about 3
    inches in diameter

1. Combine eggs with remaining filling ingredients.

2. Fill and roll pancakes. Hold each pancake closed with a toothpick.

Makes 24 pieces

STEAK TARTAR

½ pound fillet of beef, ground
1 small onion, finely chopped
2 tablespoons capers
2 anchovies, chopped
1 egg yolk
Freshly ground pepper to taste
24 thin crepe-type pancakes, about 3
    inches in diameter
Fresh parsley for garnish

1. Combine all of the filling ingredients and toss lightly.

2. Place 1 tablespoon of the filling in the center of each pancake, roll up, and hold with a toothpick. Garnish with fresh parsley.

Makes 24 pieces

TABBOULEH

1½ cups bulgur wheat (also called
  wheat pilaf)
1½ cups water
⅓ cup light salad or olive oil
1 teaspoon dried mint
½ cup finely chopped yellow or red
  onions
1 cup fresh parsley, chopped
1 large tomato, chopped
⅓–½ cup fresh lemon juice

24 thin crepe-type pancakes, about 5
  inches in diameter

1. Combine bulgur wheat with water,
salad oil, and mint. Let stand one-half
hour.

2. Add the other filling ingredients,
mix well, and refrigerate at least 2
hours. Fill and roll up pancakes.

Makes 24 pieces

TAMARA

This savory paste of Greek origin is usually served on bread or crackers. We
decided to wrap it up in a pancake.

3 slices white bread
4 tablespoons tamara (canned carp roe
  or other roe will do)
¼ cup fresh lemon juice
½ cup fresh parsley, chopped fine
¾ cup olive oil
24 thin crepe-type pancakes, about 3
  inches in diameter

1. Trim crusts from bread and soak
slices in cold water. Squeeze out water.

2. Place bread, tamara, lemon juice,
and parsley in blender. Blend 30
seconds at high speed.

3. Gradually add olive oil. The
mixture should be the consistency of
mayonnaise.

4. Place 1 tablespoon of the mixture
on each pancake. Roll up and hold in
place with toothpick.

Makes 24 pieces

ASPARAGUS VINAIGRETTE

*16 fresh young asparagus spears, cut
off about 5 inches from the tip*
*1 cup Vinaigrette Sauce with Fresh Dill
(see page 94, Sauces)*
Freshly ground pepper to taste
*8 thin Lemon Crepe Pancakes, about 5
inches in diameter (see page 24)*
1 cup sour cream or yogurt

1. Steam asparagus spears for no more than 8 minutes.

2. Place asparagus spears in vinaigrette sauce for several hours, or refrigerate overnight.

3. Sprinkle spears with fresh pepper, and let stand at room temperature for at least 1 hour before rolling 2 spears in each pancake.

4. Serve in a dish with sour cream or yogurt.

Serves 8

MANICOTTI

*T*his is one of those light Italian first course dishes that stimulates the taste buds to wish for more. Although traditionally a nonmeat dish, we enjoy it with a little pepperoni chopped up in the sauce.

FILLING

¾ *cup ricotta cheese*
¾ *cup mozzarella cheese, cubed*
8 thin pancakes, about 5 inches in diameter

SAUCE

1½ cups tomato puree
1 tablespoon oregano
1 teaspoon fresh minced garlic or garlic powder
¼ *cup sliced pepperoni, chopped (optional)*

¼ *cup Parmesan or Romano cheese, finely grated*

1. Combine ricotta and mozzarella cheeses and mix thoroughly.

2. Place about 2 tablespoons of the cheese mixture on each pancake and roll up. Place in a buttered baking dish seam side down.

3. Combine all sauce ingredients in a pan and simmer until heated through.

4. Pour sauce over the manicotti and bake in a 350°F. oven for about 20 minutes. Garnish with the Parmesan or Romano cheese before serving.

Serves 4

65

MEXICAN ENCHILADAS

*M*exican food is distinctive and delicious, and sometimes the desire for it can be overwhelming. Tortillas for making tacos are readily available in most supermarkets, but soft tortillas for making enchiladas are not so common. Here is a recipe for enchiladas that works well with any of our thin pancake recipes, but is especially good with the cornmeal-based pancakes.

FILLING

¾ pound chopped lean beef
¼ cup red onion, chopped
½ tablespoon fresh minced garlic or garlic powder
2 tablespoons chili powder (more or less, to taste)
1 tablespoon cumin powder (optional)
½ cup Monterey Jack or sharp cheddar cheese, grated

8 thin tortilla pancakes, about 5 inches in diameter

SAUCE

1½ cups tomato puree
½ teaspoon cayenne pepper (more or less, to taste)
2 teaspoons granulated sugar

66

1. In a frying pan, sauté beef until cooked through. Drain off fat. Add all other filling ingredients and simmer over low heat, mixing well, until cheese begins to melt.

2. Place about 2 tablespoons of filling on each pancake and roll up. Place seam side down in a buttered baking dish.

3. Combine all sauce ingredients in a pan and simmer until well heated and homogenous. Pour sauce over enchiladas and bake in a 350°F. oven for about 20 minutes.

Makes 8 enchiladas

AUNT MARY'S WELSH RAREBIT

*T*his recipe comes from Sherry's Aunt Mary and is a long-standing favorite of the LaFollette family. It makes a great light lunch, too.

2 tablespoons butter or margarine
1 pound sharp cheddar cheese, cubed
1 cup beer
1 egg
1 tablespoon Dijon mustard
1 tablespoon Worcestershire sauce
8 thick Johnny Cakes or 12 crumpets,
    Bannocks, or Scones (see pages 31,
    36, 30, 38)

1. In double boiler, heat water in lower section to heat butter or margarine in top. Add cheddar to butter, stirring until it melts.

2. Gradually add beer to cheese mixture.

3. Beat egg, Dijon mustard, and Worcestershire slightly with fork or whisk. Add 3-4 tablespoons of melted cheese mixture. Beat a bit more.

4. Slowly combine egg mixture into cheese, stirring well. Do not allow water to boil or egg will curdle!

5. Spoon the rarebit over hot pancakes, and enjoy.

Serves 4-6

67

RUSSIAN BLINIS
HORS D'OEUVRES

*B*linis are light and crisp little edible plates for holding a variety of delicious combinations of finger food. Here are a few of the traditional Russian toppings—but once you've got the plate, you can put almost anything on it. Raid your refrigerator—be inventive—go on a blini binge. For the batter recipe, see page 35, Russian Blinis.

BLINIS WITH CAVIAR AND SOUR CREAM

½ cup fine grade red or black caviar
12 blinis
½ lemon for juice
½ cup sour cream

Place a tablespoon of caviar on each blini and squeeze a little lemon juice on top; then add a dollop of sour cream.

BLINIS WITH CHOPPED EGG AND ONION

3 hard-boiled eggs, chopped
¼ cup red onion, chopped fine
¼ sour cream
1 tablespoon chopped chives
12 blinis
Paprika for garnish

In a bowl, combine topping ingredients and mix well. Spread on each blini and garnish with a sprinkling of paprika.

Makes 12 blinis

68

8
LUNCH
AND
DINNER
PANCAKES

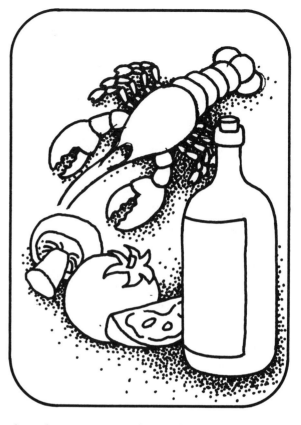

A great many North Americans never seem to consider the pancake as a candidate for a main course dish. We hope to change all that. If you have ever enjoyed Mu Shu Pork in mandarin pancakes, or Russian Chicken Kiev, or Italian veal cannelloni, or French seafood crepes then you know just how delicious and important pancakes can be as an entrée. North Americans have enjoyed Mexican tortillas with any number of fillings— but just never think of a tortilla as a pancake, let alone a pancake that they can prepare at home.

Well, one of the purposes of this book is to change your mind about pancakes being for breakfast only. In this chapter you will find recipes for delicious, satisfying, and easy-to-prepare dishes that can be served for both lunch and the main course of a dinner.

BEEF STROGANOFF

*E*very Russian restaurant worth its salt and sour cream will have beef Stroganoff on the menu. This delicious concoction, supposedly created by the epicure Count Stroganoff during the reign of the Romanov czars, really demands prime beef.

2 tablespoons shallots, minced
2 tablespoons butter or margarine
2 tablespoons flour
½ cup beef bouillon
¼ cup dry red wine
¼ cup sour cream
1 tablespoon capers
Freshly ground pepper to taste
1 cup prime cooked beef, cut into ½-
    inch cubes
¼ cup sliced fresh mushrooms
8 thin crepe-type pancakes, about 5
    inches in diameter

70

1. Sauté shallots in melted butter or margarine. Stir in two tablespoons flour to make a thick paste. Gradually add the bouillon, then wine, then sour cream. Do not boil! Add capers and freshly ground pepper to taste. Adjust seasonings if necessary. Add beef and mushrooms to sauce and heat through.

2. Fill and roll pancakes. Place rolled pancakes in a buttered dish, seam side down, and bake at 350°F. for about 15 minutes, or until heated through.

Serves 4

BREAST OF CHICKEN WITH PROSCIUTTO

4 chicken breasts
8 slices prosciutto
⅓ cup fresh mushrooms, sliced
2 tablespoons Dijon mustard
½ cup freshly grated parmesan cheese
Freshly ground black pepper to taste
1 cup Basic Bechamel Sauce (see page 95)
8 thin crepe-type pancakes, about 5 inches in diameter

1. Bring 1 quart water to a boil in a large sauce pan. Add chicken breasts and simmer for 30 minutes. Cool.

2. Remove bones and skin chicken breasts; halve each breast, so that you now have 8 pieces of chicken. Now fill and roll pancakes, first layering a slice of prosciutto, then a section of chicken breast, then a few sliced mushrooms. Roll. Place, seam down, in buttered casserole.

3. Add Dijon mustard, Parmesan, and freshly ground pepper to basic bechamel sauce. Pour over pancakes.

4. Preheat oven to 350°F. Bake for about ½ hour, or until sauce is bubbling.

Serves 4

71

CHICKEN A LA RITZ

1 cup of diced cooked chicken
½ cup dry sherry
½ cup fresh or frozen broccoli, chopped
¼ cup minced yellow onions
½ cup Basic Bechamel Sauce (see page 95)
Freshly ground pepper to taste
8 thin crepe-type pancakes, about 5 inches in diameter

1. Marinate diced cooked chicken in dry sherry for at least 2 hours. Reserve sherry marinade and chicken.

2. Prepare broccoli, cooking no more than 3-4 minutes if fresh, or 6-8 minutes if frozen. Combine with marinated chicken, and set aside.

3. Prepare basic bechamel sauce, sautéing the onions in the butter or margarine as you melt it. Add the reserved sherry marinade to ½ cup of basic bechamel sauce, adding more sherry if needed. Add pepper to taste.

4. Add chicken and broccoli to sauce to complete filling. Fill and roll pancakes.

Serves 4

72

CHICKEN ALMONDINE

2 tablespoons shallots, chopped
½ cup Basic Bechamel Sauce (see page 95)
½ cup chicken stock, preferably homemade
2 tablespoons tomato puree
¼ cup dry sherry
2 tablespoons slivered almonds
1 tablespoon Dijon mustard
1 teaspoon dried tarragon
Fresh ground pepper to taste
¾ cup diced cooked chicken
8 thin Lemon Crepe Pancakes, about 5 inches in diameter (see page 24)

1. Prepare basic bechamel sauce, sautéing the shallots in the butter or margarine as you melt it. Add all other sauce ingredients to ½ cup of the bechamel sauce; then add chicken, and simmer for a few minutes. Let stand until cool.

2. Place 2 tablespoons of the filling on each pancake and roll up. Place pancakes in a buttered dish, seam side down.

3. Bake in a 350°F. oven for about 15 minutes, or until heated through.

Serves 4

CHICKEN KIEV

2 chicken breasts

1 egg

⅛ cup vegetable oil

2 tablespoons chives, fresh chopped or
   dried

2 tablespoons parsley, fresh chopped or
   dried

1 tablespoon Dijon mustard

Freshly ground black pepper to taste

8 thin crepe-type pancakes, 5–6 inches
   in diameter

1. Place chicken breasts in pan of boiling water and cook for 10–15 minutes until cooked through. Do not overcook.

2. When chicken has cooled, remove the meat from the bone, skin, and slice into thin strips about an inch long.

3. Beat the egg and oil together in a bowl. Add the chives, parsley, mustard, and pepper. Mix well, then toss in the chicken strips.

4. Place about 2 tablespoons of this mixture in the center of each pancake. Roll up and place in a buttered baking dish, seam side down. Bake at 350°F. for 20 minutes.

Serves 4

73

CHICKEN WITH WALNUTS AND GREEN GRAPES

¾ cup cooked chicken, cut into ½-inch
   cubes

½ cup green grapes, halved

⅓ cup chopped walnuts

½ cup commercial mayonnaise

2 tablespoons Dijon mustard

1 teaspoon dried parsley, or ¼ cup
   fresh parsley

1 hard-boiled egg, chopped

Freshly ground pepper to taste

8 thin Lemon Crepe Pancakes, about 5
   inches in diameter (see page 24)

Combine all filling ingredients. Place ¼ cup of filling in the center of each pancake and roll up. Place on plate seam side down, and serve at room temperature. (This dish can be prepared ahead of time and refrigerated for a few hours.)

Serves 4

COQUILLE ST. JACQUES

½ pound small bay scallops
½ cup dry vermouth or white wine
¼ cup minced shallots
½ cup Basic Bechamel Sauce (see page 95)
¼ cup freshly choped parsley
1 tablespoon Dijon mustard
Freshly grated parmesan cheese to taste
½ cup sliced fresh mushrooms
8 thin crepe-type pancakes, about 5 inches in diameter

1. Simmer scallops in vermouth or white wine for 3 minutes. Reserve liquid and scallops.

2. Prepare basic bechamel sauce, sautéing shallots in butter or margarine as you melt it. Add reserved wine and all other sauce ingredients to ½ cup of the bechamel sauce.

3. Add scallops and mushrooms to sauce to complete filling. Place ¼ cup of filling in the center of each pancake and roll up.

4. Place rolled pancakes in a buttered dish, seam side down, and heat in a 350°F. oven for about 10 minutes, or until heated through.

Serves 4

74

GERMAN POTATO PANCAKES

1 cup red potatoes, cooked and cubed
½ cup mayonnaise
¼ cup plain yogurt
¼ cup Dijon mustard
¼ cup crisp crumbled bacon, or diced ham
¼ cup chopped celery
Fresh ground pepper to taste
8 thin crepe-type pancakes, about 5 inches in diameter

1. Combine all the filling ingredients.

2. Place ½ cup of the filling in the center of each pancake and roll up.

3. Place the rolled pancakes in a buttered dish, seam side down, and bake in a 350°F. oven for 10 minutes, or until heated through.

Serves 4

LAMB CURRY

¼ cup chopped yellow onions

¼ cup butter or margarine

2 tablespoons curry powder (or to taste)

2 tablespoons flour

1 cup broth, preferably homemade lamb (or beef)

1½ cups cooked lamb, cut into ½-inch cubes

½ cup canned Italian plum tomatoes, drained

½ cup dried chopped apples

8 thin crepe-type pancakes, about 5 inches in diameter

1. Sauté onions in butter or margarine.

2. Add curry powder and flour. Mix well with wire whisk or wooden spoon.

3. Gradually add broth. Stir until thick and smooth.

4. Add lamb, tomatoes, and chopped dried apples. Mix well and place ¼ cup of the lamb curry on each pancake. Roll up and place in a buttered dish, seam side down.

5. Place in a 350°F. oven for about 10 minutes, or until heated through.

Note: Plain yogurt and chutney may be served as condiments with this dish.

Serves 4

75

LASAGNA

1 pound ground beef

4 tablespoons butter or margarine

3 cups Nice and Spicy Tomato Sauce
    (see page 97)

2 cups ricotta or cottage cheese

1 cup chopped, fresh spinach
    (optional)

8 ounces mozzarella cheese, shredded

8 ounces freshly grated parmesan
    cheese (more or less)

16 thin crepe-type pancakes, about 5
    inches in diameter

1. Preheat oven to 350°F.

2. Sauté beef in butter or margarine. When brown but not crusty, drain and remove meat to warm platter. Wipe out pan with paper towel.

3. Prepare tomato sauce. Simmer at least 1 hour. Combine and add ricotta and cottage cheeses, beef, and spinach to tomato sauce. You are now ready to assemble Lasagna.

4. Pour approximately 1 cup of sauce on bottom of a 13″ × 9″ × 2″ casserole. Add 5-6 pancakes, then a layer of the mozzarella and Swiss cheeses, and finally, a sprinkling of the freshly grated Parmesan. Repeat the steps twice more.

5. Bake for approximately 30 minutes, or until bubbling. Allow to stand about 10 minutes before serving.

Serves 6

76

LOBSTER SUPREME

¾ cup Basic Bechamel Sauce (see page 95)

¼ cup Pernod or brandy

6 ounces fresh, canned, or frozen lobster meat, chopped

1 avocado pear, quartered and sliced thin

⅓ cup scallions (including greens), finely chopped

2 tablespoons tomato puree

8 thin Lemon Crepe Pancakes, about 5 inches in diameter (see page 24)

1. Prepare basic bechamel sauce. To ¾ cup of sauce, add the Pernod or brandy; then add remaining filling ingredients and mix well.

2. Place ¼ cup of filling in the center of each pancake and roll up.

3. Place rolled-up pancakes in a buttered baking dish, seam side down. Extra filling may be spooned on top.

4. Bake in a 350°F. oven for 10 minutes, or until heated through.

Serves 4

SAVORY SATE

1 cup lean cooked pork, cut into ½-inch cubes

⅓ cup peanut butter

3 tablespoons soy sauce

3 tablespoons fresh lemon juice

2 cloves garlic, finely chopped

⅓ cup shallots, finely chopped

1 teaspoon ground cumin

1 teaspoon ground coriander

1 teaspoon ground ginger

2 tablespoons ground Brazil nuts (optional)

8 thin Lemon Crepe Pancakes, about 5 inches in diameter (see page 24)

1. Marinate pork in the remaining filling ingredients. Mix and toss well. Refrigerate at least overnight, tossing pork in marinade 3 or 4 times.

2. Fill and roll pancakes. Serve cold.

Note: A dollop of mint or currant jelly goes well with these savory sate pancakes.

Serves 4

77

VEAL CANNELLONI

¼ *cup onion, chopped*
2 *tablespoons margarine or butter*
¾ *pound veal cutlet, sliced thin*
¾ *cup sour cream*
1 *tablespoon fresh minced garlic or*
    garlic powder
1 *tablespoon oregano*
¼ *cup prosciutto, sliced thin and cut*
    into strips about an inch long
Freshly ground pepper to taste
8 *thin Cannelloni pancakes, about 5*
    inches in diameter (see page 24)

1. In a frying pan, sauté onion in margarine or butter. When onion just begins to crisp around the edges, remove with a slotted spoon and sauté veal, about 3 minutes on each side.

2. When cool, slice the veal into thin strips about an inch long.

3. Mix all filling ingredients together in a bowl.

4. Place about 2 tablespoons of the filling in the center of each pancake. Roll up and place in a buttered baking dish, seam side down. Bake at 350°F. for 20 minutes.

Serves 4

78

MEXICAN TACOS

8 fresh tortillas, or other thin pancakes
¾ pound lean chopped beef
¼ cup tomato puree
¼ cup red onion, chopped fine
2 tablespoons dried chili powder (or
*   more)*
½ teaspoon cayenne pepper (more or
*   less)*
½ cup sharp cheddar cheese, grated

1. Fold the pancakes in half; place them in a baking dish and crisp them in a 350°F. oven for ten minutes.

2. Sauté the chopped beef in a well-greased hot frying pan until cooked through. Drain and remove fat. Add the tomato puree, onion, chili, and cayenne to the chopped meat. If the mixture is too dry, add a little more tomato puree. Sauté for about five minutes so that the flavors will blend; stir occasionally.

3. Remove the folded pancakes from the oven. Fill with about 2 tablespoons of the mixture, top with grated cheese, and replace in the baking dish, open side up. Bake in a 350°F. oven for about 10 minutes, or until the cheese has melted.

Makes 8 tacos

79

MU SHU PORK

1 cup cooked lean pork or chicken,
* diced*
⅓ cup dry sherry or rice wine
2 eggs
2 tablespoons soy sauce
¼ cup bamboo shoots, chopped
¼ cup bean sprouts
¼ cup fresh mushrooms, chopped
8 mandarin or other thin pancakes,
* about 5 inches in diameter*
¼ cup scallion greens, sliced thin
Duck sauce and Chinese mustard, to
* taste*

1. Marinate pork or chicken in sherry or rice wine for a few hours; overnight is fine.

2. Beat eggs. Cook eggs like a crepe in a lightly greased hot frying pan, then turn and cook other side. When cool, slice eggs into thin strips.

3. In the same well greased hot frying pan, add the meat and marinade, and sauté for a few moments, stirring constantly. Add soy sauce, bamboo shoots, bean sprouts, egg strips, and mushrooms. Sauté for few more moments until heated through. Stir continuously.

4. Place 2 tablespoons of the mixture in the center of a pancake, add some of the scallion greens, Chinese mustard, and/or duck sauce to taste, and roll up and eat with your fingers. Each person makes his or her own filled pancake.

Serves 4

80

9
DESSERT PANCAKES

Crepes Suzette, Drambuie Towers, Sicilian Cannellonis—the names conjure up visions of rare, exotic dishes. However, the basic element in all of these desserts is the pancake.

Dessert is the final act of any meal—it should be both dramatic and satisfying. The recipes that follow glorify the pancake: rolled in sweet confections, doused with a variety of liqueurs, and sometimes served flambeau. Some will be rolled and filled like Sicilian cannellonis. Some will be served flat, but topped with a variety of sauces like Marrons Glaces, Zabaglione, or Cherries Jubilee. Others will be stacked, with custard or fruit fillings between the layers, to make what the French call a Crepe Gateau and the Italians call Zuppa Inglese. In any language, these pancake combinations make simple, delicious, and unusual desserts.

These recipes will specify the best kind of pancake to be used: thin for rolling, normal and thick for stacking. Sometimes we will be exact, limiting the choice to only one or two pancake recipes; generally, however, we will leave the choice up to you. You are the one preparing this food; make the meal reflect your own personal taste.

APRICOT MOUSSE

*A*pricots and yogurt trace their roots east to Asia. *Mousse* means *foam* in French. This east–west blend of flavorful foam makes a rich but refreshing filling for a rolled crepe dessert.

1 cup tinned apricots, drained
½ cup granulated sugar
½ cup plain yogurt
¼ cup Cointreau, or liqueur of your choice
4 eggs, separated
8 thin Hungarian Palacsinta or Lemon Crepe Pancakes, about 5 inches in diameter (see pages 23–24)

82

1. Place apricots, sugar, yogurt, liqueur, and egg yolks in a blender or food processor, and blend at high speed for about 30 seconds.

2. Beat egg whites in a bowl until stiff.

3. Pour the blended mixture into a large bowl, and fold the beaten egg whites in gently.

4. Place about three tablespoons of the mousse in the center of each pancake and fold over. Serve at once.

Note: For a variation, reserve the Cointreau and pour over the filled pancakes.

Serves 8

BAKED ALASKA, GRAND MARNIER

Baked Alaska is one of the most dramatic and surprising desserts imaginable. How does that ice cream stay frozen? It is also a lesson in the power of insulation.

Meringue
4 egg whites
½ cup granulated sugar
8 thin Lemon Crepe Pancakes, about 5
*   inches in diameter (see page 24)*
⅓ cup Grand Marnier
1 round pint vanilla ice cream, straight
*   from the freezer*
¼ cup brandy

1. Preheat oven to 450°F.

2. Beat egg whites until they form soft peaks, then beat in sugar, one tablespoon at a time, to form a meringue.

3. Place one pancake in an ovenproof dish, then a tablespoon of Grand Marnier. With a warm knife, cut a slice of ice cream and place on top of the pancake. Continue until you have a stack of pancakes soaked in Grand Marnier, separated by discs of ice cream. Using a spatula, cover the entire form with the meringue. Place in the oven for 5 minutes, or until golden brown. Splash on the brandy, ignite, and serve.

Serves 4

BANANA BLANKETS

*T*hese are so simple and so good—and yet we've never seen them anywhere outside our own house. We hope you will change that. Both pancakes and bananas tend to be taken for granted as nothing very special. Combined in this recipe they become a memorable and dramatic finale to any evening meal.

¾ cup fresh orange juice
¼ cup fresh lemon juice
Zest from one lemon skin
½ cup brown or white sugar
½ teaspoon ground cinnamon
3 tablespoons margarine or butter
8 small ripe bananas, or 4 large ones
    cut in half
8 thin Hungarian Palacsinta or Lemon
    Crepe Pancakes, about 5 inches in
    diameter (see pages 23–24)
½ cup dark rum or brandy

1. Preheat oven to 350°F.

2. Combine juices, zest, sugar, cinnamon, and margarine or butter in a saucepan. Simmer until margarine has melted and sugar is completely dissolved. Stir occasionally.

3. While sauce is cooking, roll bananas in pancakes.

4. Coat the bottom of an ovenproof dish with margarine. Place the pancakes in dish seam side down, cover with sauce, and bake for 20–30 minutes.

5. Remove from oven, pour rum or brandy over the banana blankets, ignite, and serve flambeau.

Serves 8

BLACK FOREST CREPE TORTE

A pancake version of a famous old German dessert recipe.

2 ounces dark semisweet chocolate
1 tablespoon butter or margarine
¼ cup milk
¼ cup water
¼ cup flour
2 large eggs
2 cups heavy cream
⅓ cup granulated sugar
1 cup first-rate cherry jam
¼ cup kirsch
12 thin Hungarian Palacsinta or
*   Lemon Crepe Pancakes, about 5*
*   inches in diameter (see pages*
*   23-24)*

1. Melt chocolate and butter or margarine in top of double boiler.

Cool. Combine with milk, water, flour, and eggs in blender. Refrigerate sauce until you are ready to assemble torte. You will have enough sauce for approximately 12 pancakes.

2. Whip cream until it forms stiff peaks. Combine with sugar, jam, and kirsch.

3. Assemble torte with the chocolate mixture between pancakes until all 12 pancakes are stacked one on top of the other. Spoon the cream, jam, and kirsch mixture over the top and let it run down the sides—rich and delicious! (The torte can be made in advance and refrigerated for a few hours.)

Serves 8

BLUEBERRY BLINTZES

*B*lintzes can be served as an hors d'oeuvre (see page 61) or as a dessert. Sweetened cottage cheese is the traditional filling, often with the addition of fruits and nuts. This is our favorite.

1 cup cottage cheese
¼ cup granulated sugar
¼ teaspoon vanilla extract
¾ cup fresh blueberries (or frozen, defrosted)
8 blintzes (see page 25) or other thin pancake, about 5 inches in diameter

1. Place the cottage cheese, sugar, and vanilla in a bowl and blend together with a large spoon. Add the blueberries and continue mixing until blueberries are equally distributed.

2. Place about 2 tablespoons of the filling in the center of the uncooked side of a blintze. Fold the four edges of the blintze toward the center and turn the blintze over.

3. Place all the blintzes seam side down in a well-buttered frying pan. Cook until golden brown on the bottom; turn and cook the other side until heated through.

Serves 8

86

CHOCOLATE RUM FRUIT

*T*his filling combines three of our favorite flavors in one delightfully rich—yet fresh—rolled crepe dessert. Make sure you use chocolate chips made with real chocolate. The "chocolate flavored" variety are nowhere near the same.

1 cup chocolate chips
½ cup heavy cream
¼ cup dark rum
8 thin Hungarian Palacsinta or Lemon Crepe Pancakes, about 5 inches in diameter (see pages 23-24)
1 cup fresh fruit: green grapes, berries, diced pineapple, or a mixture of your own choosing

1. Place chocolate chips in a double boiler with the water at a high simmer, just below boiling.

2. When the chips around the edges begin to melt, pour in the heavy cream. After about two more minutes, begin to stir the mixture. Continue periodic stirring until the mixture is well blended.

3. Add rum and stir briefly to distribute the flavor. Remove from heat and set aside to cool.

4. Place about 2 tablespoons of chocolate sauce in the center of each pancake. Place a selection of fresh fruit in the sauce and roll up the pancake. These can be eaten out of hand or served on a plate. We sometimes serve the pancakes, the sauce, and the fruit separately and let everybody fix their own, selecting the fruit that pleases them most.

Serves 8

87

CREPES SUZETTE

*T*here are a number of stories as to how this most famous crepe dish got its name. We like the one where it was invented by mistake: It happened in Paris. A 14-year-old assistant pastry chef, while preparing a butter, orange, and liqueur crepe sauce over the fire, somehow managed to ignite the sauce. Seized by a sudden mix of terror and inspiration, he served the dish in its flaming state. Among the guests being served was Prince Albert of England. He was so delighted that he immediately named the dish in honor of the host's daughter, who just happened to be about the same age as the assistant pastry chef.

¼ cup butter or margarine
½ cup granulated sugar
Zest from ½ an orange skin
Juice from one orange
1 jigger Curacao or Triple Sec liqueur
*   (scant ¼ cup)*
8 Lemon Crepe Pancakes, about 5
*   inches in diameter (see page 24)*
1 jigger Grand Marnier
1 jigger kirsch
1 jigger brandy

1. Place butter in a large, heavy pan and melt it over a low flame. When the butter is melted, add the sugar and stir until it, too, has melted. Then add the zest, the orange juice, and the jigger of curacao.

2. Roll the crepes into tight cylinders and place in the Suzette sauce. Spoon the sauce over them, if necessary.

3. When heated through, add the remaining liqueurs. Ignite and serve.

Serves 8

DRAMBUIE TOWERS

*A*ncient castle towers rising above craggy highlands—that is the image of Scotland that often comes to mind. Our towers are built of Scotch Drop Scones (see page 39) mortared with marmalade, and doused with Drambuie. They may not match the image, but they are delicious to eat.

½ cup Drambuie, or other liqueur of
*   your choice*
8 Scotch Drop Scones, about 3-4 inches
*   in diameter (crumpets, blinis, or*
*   other small, thick pancakes can*
*   also be used in this recipe)*
¼ cup orange marmalade (or less)

1. Spoon a tablespoon, or more, of Drambuie over a scone. Use enough to really soak the scone. Spread orange marmalade over the scone. Place another scone on top and repeat the process until you have made a tower 8 scones high. Pour any remaining Drambuie over the top.

2. Serve at once, or refrigerate briefly before serving.

Serves 8

GRANNY ICE CONES

*K*ids love these. George's mother used to make them back in the '50s when freezer units first became popular. They are easy to make and fun to eat!

¾ cup granulated sugar
1 banana
Juice of one orange
Juice and 2 tablespoons zest of one
*   lemon*
½ cup water
8 thin Hungarian Palacsinta pancakes,
*   about 5 inches in diameter (see*
*   page 23)*

1. Place sugar, banana, orange and lemon juices, and water in blender. Blend; then fold in zest. Freeze in ice tray, or any other suitable container.

2. When frozen, place about ¼ cup on each pancake. Roll into cone shape and freeze again.

Makes 8 cones

PEACH MELBA

*T*he mix of peach and raspberry flavors was a favorite of the world-famous opera star, Nellie Melba. Legend has it that the equally world-famous French chef, Auguste Escoffier, first created a peach and raspberry dessert with vanilla ice cream and named it Peach Melba in Nellie's honor. Actually, Nellie's last name was Mitchell, but since she was born in Melbourne, Australia, she took the stage name of Melba. So when you serve a peach melba you are honoring not only a great opera star, but a great French chef, and a great Australian city as well.

1 cup raspberries, fresh or frozen (but defrosted)
½ cup granulated sugar
8 thin pancakes, 5 inches in diameter
8 slices tinned cling peaches
1½ cups vanilla ice cream
¾ framboise (raspberry) liqueur, or brandy

1. Place the raspberries and sugar in a blender or food processor, and blend at high speed for about 30 seconds. (Raspberry jam may be substituted.)

2. Place 2 tablespoons of the raspberry puree in the center of each pancake. Place a peach slice on top and roll the pancake over the filling. Place 2 rolled and filled pancakes in each serving dish.

3. Top each serving with vanilla ice cream and framboise liqueur.

Serves 8

SICILIAN CANNELLONI

*T*his unique mix of ingredients, credited to the Sicilians, is one of our favorites.

1 cup ricotta cheese
½ cup granulated sugar
¼ cup rum, or Amaretto, or other liqueur
½ teaspoon ground cinnamon
Zest from ½ lemon rind
⅓ cup chocolate chips
8 thin pancakes, about 5 inches in diameter
¼ cup powdered sugar

1. Combine ricotta cheese, sugar, and half of the rum in a bowl; mix with a spoon. When you have a homogenous mixture, add the cinnamon, zest, and chocolate chips and blend briefly.

2. Place a scant ¼ cup of the filling in the center of each pancake and roll up.

3. Place two filled pancakes seam side down on each serving plate. Pour the remaining rum over each serving and dust with the powdered sugar.

Serves 8

91

SPICED APPLE CREAM

*I*t was in the 1950s that blenders started sprouting on kitchen counters and George's mother started making her own ice cream concoctions. They usually came out solid as a rock or filled with ice chips. However, this one was particularly good, once melted somewhat. We have adapted it to make a creamy, spicy, fresh crepe filling.

1 large apple, cored and diced, with the skin on
1 cup of heavy cream
½ cup granulated sugar
Juice and zest of one lemon
½ teaspoon powdered cinnamon
½ teaspoon powdered ginger or allspice
8 thin Hungarian Palacsinta or Lemon Crepe Pancakes, about 5 inches in diameter (see pages 23–24)

1. Place all filling ingredients in a blender or food processor, and blend at high speed for about 30 seconds.

2. Spread the mixture over each pancake and roll it up. Place pancake, seam side down, on a serving plate. Continue until all eight pancakes are arranged on the plate. Pour any remaining sauce over the pancakes. Serve at once, or refrigerate until ready to serve.

Serves 8

92

ZUPPA INGLESE

*H*ow this unique dessert ever got dubbed "Soup of the English" is a great mystery. It has become completely Italian in the transition and is a quite marvelous way to end a meal.

½ cup sour cream

¼ cup granulated sugar

Juice and zest from one lemon

3 normal basic griddle cakes, about 8 inches in diameter

1 jigger (scant ¼ cup) of Sambucca liqueur

1 jigger Amaretto liqueur

1 jigger marsala wine (any one of these liqueurs can be used, or a liqueur of your choice)

¼ cup finely chopped candied fruit, chopped nuts, or candied sprinkles (or a mixture)

1. In a bowl, blend the sour cream, sugar, lemon juice, and lemon zest to make a uniform mixture.

2. Place one pancake in a shallow dish and pour the Sambucca liqueur over it. Then spread about ⅓ of the sour cream mixture over the pancake. Place another pancake on top and pour the Amaretto liqueur over this one, then spread the sour cream. Continue with the third pancake, marsala wine, and sour cream.

3. Sprinkle the candied fruit and/or chopped nuts over the top. Either serve at once, or refrigerate for a few hours until you are ready to serve the Zuppa Inglese.

Serves 8

93

10
SAUCES

In this chapter we include both piquant sauces for hors d'oeuvres and entrées, and sweet sauces for desserts.

In many filled and rolled pancake dishes the sauce is an essential element, binding the ingredients together while distributing flavors and seasonings throughout the filling.

In many stacked and layered dessert pancake dishes the sauce is also essential to add taste and texture, to sweeten, and sometimes to dramatically flame the dessert dish.

BASIC BECHAMEL PIQUANT SAUCE

2 tablespoons butter or margarine
2 tablespoons flour
¾ cup half and half (or heavy cream,
    sour cream, or yogurt)
¼ cup dry vermouth or white wine

1. Melt butter or margarine over low heat. Stir with wire whisk or wooden spoon.

2. Add flour and stir to make thick paste, about one minute.

3. Slowly add half and half (or combination), stirring constantly until thick and smooth. Add wine and stir in.

4. Simmer at low heat for about 15 minutes. The sauce is now ready. Add other ingredients of your choice for pancake sauces or fillings.

Makes about 1¼ cups sauce

BLENDER MAYONNAISE

1 whole egg
1 cup salad oil (approximately)
1 tablespoon Dijon mustard
1 teaspoon dried herbs (we like dill
    weed best)
⅓ cup fresh lemon juice (or to taste)

1. Break egg into blender. Add ¼ cup oil, mustard, and herbs of your choice.

2. On slowest speed, immediately—but *slowly*—add remaining oil in a steady stream. Add lemon juice to taste.

Makes about 1¼ cups sauce

BLENDER HOLLANDAISE

3 egg yolks
3 tablespoons lemon juice
½ cup parsley, chopped
½ cup butter or margarine

1. Place yolks, lemon juice, and parsley in blender.

2. Heat butter or margarine to bubbling stage. Do not allow to brown!

3. Add melted butter to yolks, lemon juice, and parsley in steady stream. Blend until mixture thickens.

Makes about 1¼ cups sauce

MARINARA

1 cup yellow onions, chopped
2 cloves garlic, minced
¼ cup olive oil
2 cups tomato puree
½ cup dry red wine
2 anchovies, chopped
1 teaspoon dried basil
½ teaspoon oregano

1 bay leaf, crumbled
Freshly ground pepper to taste

1. Sauté onions and garlic in olive oil until golden.

2. Add remaining ingredients and simmer for one hour.

Makes about 4 cups sauce

96

VINAIGRETTE SAUCE

¾ cup peanut or fine imported olive oil
¼ cup fine vinegar (we prefer balsamic)
¼ cup fresh dill, or 1 tablespoon dried
1 tablespoon Dijon-type mustard
2 tablespoons finely chopped shallots
    (optional)

Freshly ground pepper to taste

1. Combine all ingredients.
2. Stir or shake well.

Makes 1 cup sauce

NICE AND SPICY TOMATO SAUCE

2 tablespoons yellow onions, chopped
⅓ cup butter or margarine
1 cup tomato puree
¼ cup dry red wine
1 tablespoon Dijon-type mustard
¼ teaspoon oregano
¼ teaspoon basil
1 bay leaf
Freshly ground pepper to taste

1. Sauté onion in butter until limp but not brown.

2. Add other ingredients and simmer over low heat at least 30 minutes. Be sure to remove bay leaf before serving.

Note: With the addition of horseradish to taste, this sauce is also delicious served cold over seafood.

Makes about 1½ cups sauce

97

CHERRIES JUBILEE

1½ cups tinned pitted cherries, drained
½ cup kirsch
¼ cup brandy

1. Place cherries in a small container. Cover with the kirsch and let stand for a few hours; overnight is fine.

2. Place marinated cherries in a flameproof dish, add the brandy, ignite, and serve flaming over the pancakes.

Makes about 2½ cups sauce

BUTTERSCOTCH SAUCE

1⅓ cups brown sugar
¾ cup corn syrup
3 tablespoons butter or margarine
2 tablespoons water
3 or 4 tablespoons heavy cream

1. Combine sugar, corn syrup, butter, and water in heavy saucepan. Boil for one minute. Cool.

2. Stir in cream until smooth and satiny.

Makes about 2 cups sauce

98

BLUEBERRY SAUCE

*H*eavenly with vanilla ice cream!

2 cups granulated sugar
Juice and zest of 1 large lemon
½ teaspoon cinnamon
¼ teaspoon ground ginger
1 pint blueberries

1. Combine sugar, lemon juice and zest, cinnamon, and ginger in heavy saucepan. Boil for about 8 minutes.

2. Add blueberries. When they come to a boil, reduce heat and simmer for 6–7 minutes. Cool.

Makes about 3 cups sauce

PESTO

1 cup fresh basil leaves, tightly packed
½ cup olive oil
¼ cup fresh parsley
2 large garlic cloves
⅓ cup pine nuts
½ cup freshly grated Parmesan cheese

1. Combine all ingredients in blender or food processor.

2. Process until a smooth paste is formed.

Makes about 3 cups sauce

99

FAIL-PROOF FUDGE SAUCE

4 cups sugar
1 14½-ounce can evaporated milk
¼ cup butter or margarine
1 12-ounce package chocolate chips
1 cup miniature marshmallows
2 cups walnuts, chopped

1. Combine sugar, evaporated milk, and butter in heavy saucepan. Bring to a full rolling boil that cannot be stirred down. Boil for 5 minutes.

2. Add marshmallows, chocolate chips, and nuts and stir until well blended.

Note: Sauce will turn into proper fudge in about 8 hours; however, it can always be reheated.

Makes about 4 cups sauce

MARRONS GLACES

1 cup tinned chestnuts
⅛ cup fresh lemon juice
½ cup sugar
½ cup water
¼ cup brandy

1. Place chestnuts, liquid from the chestnut can, and lemon juice in a blender or food processor, and blend at high speed until pureed.

2. Place sugar and water in a saucepan and simmer until sugar is dissolved. Stir occasionally. Add the chestnut puree and continue stirring until the mixture become a homogenous sauce.

1. Turn the flame off, add the brandy, and stir until well blended. This sauce may be served either warm or cool.

3. Turn the flame off, add the brandy,

Makes about 2½ cups sauce

STRAWBERRY SAUCE

1½ cups fresh (or frozen and defrosted) strawberries (other berries or fruit may be used)
½ cup sour cream or plain yogurt
½ cup granulated sugar
¼ cup brandy or liqueur of your choice (optional)

1. Place all ingredients in a blender or food processor, and blend at high speed.
2. Serve at once or refrigerate for a few hours.

Makes about 2½ cups sauce

ZABAGLIONE

4 eggs, separated
¾ cup confectioners sugar
⅓ cup marsala wine (sherry may be substituted)
½ teaspoon vanilla

1. Place egg yolks and half the sugar in the top of a double boiler. Beat until smooth and well blended. Add the marsala wine gradually, and continue to beat the mixture. When well blended, remove the zabaglione from the flame.
2. Add the remaining sugar and the vanilla to egg whites, and beat until stiff.
3. Serve the zabaglione over the pancakes, then place a dollop of the egg white mixture in the center.

Makes about 2½ cups sauce

INDEX